PROJECTS WITH

BIRDS

PROJECTS WITH
BIRDS

Peter Goodfellow

In Association with the British Trust for Ornithology

Foreword by *Tony Soper*

THE CROWOOD PRESS

Dedication

In memory of my grandmother, Daisy Goodfellow (1878–1980) who, when I was a teenager about to go duck-counting or wader-watching on the local estuary or creek would affectionately declare that I was 'going down the drain!'

First published in 1992 by
The Crowood Press Ltd.
Ramsbury, Marlborough
Wiltshire SN8 2HR

Line illustrations by the author and by Chris D Orr

Photograph on page 2: great spotted woodpecker.

British Library Cataloguing in Publication Data

A catalogue record for this book is available from the British Library.

ISBN 1 85223 613 2

Edited and designed by
D & N Publishing
DTP & Editorial Services
5 The Green
Baydon
Wiltshire SN8 2JW

Printed and bound by BPCC Hazell Books Ltd.

Contents

Foreword

by Tony Soper

It was in the early 1970s that I encouraged Peter Goodfellow to write for those who wanted to do more than just *watch* birds. The resulting book was an immediate success, so this new revised version is a very welcome addition to the many bird books now available, and is even more useful in the 1990s than the original.

Here is a new text, freshly illustrated, which fills the gap on the bookshelf between the field guides and the species monographs. The new birdwatcher is led from advice on keeping a notebook to detailed information on how to take part in scientific fieldwork, especially the surveys sponsored by our major national birdwatching organizations. There are practical ideas for twitchers as well as computer bird-buffs and bird gardeners. All contribute to our increasing knowledge of birds and bird behaviour, and there is no doubt that detailed long-term studies improve the quality of our conservation work.

The author is well-qualified as a guide. He is a skilled and successful field naturalist who combines the pure enjoyment of open-air bird-watching with the more academic pursuit of ornithology. He has included a useful chapter which emphasizes the vital rôle of conservation in today's birdwatching.

The rare isabelline shrike would thrill any birdwatcher who found one in Britain.

Anyone reading and acting on the projects in this book will enjoy birdwatching far more by sharing the excitement and discoveries with others. It really is important to pool our information.

So I am very pleased to recommend *Projects with Birds* to birdwatchers of all ages and experiences in the firm belief that it will increase our enjoyment of one of the most rewarding of all studies.

Tony Soper

Preface

In the story of world birds, during the time I have been a birdwatcher, several things stick in my mind: the takahe was seen again in New Zealand in 1948 after having been thought extinct for fifty years; even more striking, was the rediscovery in 1988 of Jerdon's courser which had not been recorded since 1900; I saw in England a North American bird, the myrtle warbler (as it was then known; now it is the yellow-rumped warbler) twenty-five years before I saw a European melodious warbler; I now see a peregrine several times a year; with a friend, I recorded the first breeding siskins in Devon; and avocets – the symbol of the Royal Society for the Protection of Birds (RSPB) – have wintered on my local river every year since they first appeared in the winter of 1947/8.

It is comforting to have these happy memories, but some years now pass without my seeing a barn owl; it seems an age ago that I found a red-backed shrike's nest with young; no longer can I see a wild chough in Cornwall; roseate terns rarely get in my notebook; and where have the woodlarks and cirl buntings gone? Many birdwatchers can make comparisons like this. It is not so comforting to realize that the International Council for Bird Preservation's *Red Data Book* lists over 400 kinds of birds in danger of extinction, and it is a sobering thought that one of the best-selling bird books in recent years has been the international volume *Save the Birds*, which by its very title exhorts us to do more than just watch birds. Yet library and bookshop shelves suggest watching is the thing. They are full of magazines and books to help us identify what we see, and the past decade has seen great strides in refining the watchers' skills in distinguishing species easily confused, sorting out adults from immatures, and in 'discovering' new birds for the British list.

There is happily an increasingly large number of people who do not only want to look at nature but also want to know something about what they see. Best-selling books, such as the Hamlyn and Peterson field guides, the *New Naturalist* series, and the monographs from the publishers, T & AD Poyser, are indicative of a desire to learn about bird life. We do not only want to know the name of the bird or details of its life, status and distribution. We have come to care that its very existence is safe-guarded. In 1973, in an earlier version of this book, I wrote: 'Today's concern over environmental pollution and conservation will be of no avail unless all those who are worried are able to qualify their anxiety with evidence based not only on a love of wildlife but also on some knowledge of species' life histories, ecology and habitat management.' Nearly twenty years later that concern is still today's concern.

Many people today who watch birds in their gardens, on day-trips, and when they are on holiday, are not sure how best to learn more about those birds and how best they can help to look after them. Certainly the more we know, the more powerful we shall be individually, or as a society, or as a nation, to protect the birds we love. The authors of *Save the Birds* wrote: 'A world without birds is almost unthinkable. It would certainly be uninhabitable.' This spurs me to offer this new book to direct the observer to a variety of activities – the projects – involvement in which, it is hoped, will serve three purposes: first, improve the birdwatcher's knowledge; secondly, spur him or her to think of related activities more suitable to his or her own circumstances; all of which will, thirdly in time help to save the birds.

In the pages that follow, the importance of and necessity for using a field notebook are emphasized, and then over sixty projects are outlined, dealing with basic topics, such as nests, song, food and behaviour, besides a variety of other ideas. The projects are a mixture: some are simple; and it is hoped the reader will then progress to those that are more demanding.

I am greatly indebted to the sources listed in the *Bibliography*. An additional project could well be to trace and read the original of as many of these sources as possible. Failing that, much information may be found in *A Dictionary of Birds* (ed. Campbell and Lack, 1984). This is a birdwatcher's reference library in one volume, written by many experts.

Finally, I should like to record my sincere thanks to Dr Jeremy Greenwood, the Director of the British Trust for Ornithology, and his staff, for much valued assistance; to the Wildfowl and Wetlands Trust; to Paul Walsh of the Seabirds Team; to all my birdwatching friends; to Andrew and Julie who will never let me take birdwatching too seriously; to my wife June, who has never failed to encourage me and accompany me birdwatching; and lastly, special thanks to David and Namrita for all the hours they have spent in designing and editing this book, and without whose help *Projects with Birds* would never have got into print.

Introduction

By Jeremy Greenwood, Director of the British Trust for Ornithology

Some birdwatchers are content to watch and listen to the birds they see, rewarded by the aesthetic and emotional experience. Others keep records of interesting behaviour, unusual occurrences or just the species they have seen. Such note-taking can soon develop into systematic recording and it is then that it starts to pay dividends, revealing aspects of the lives of birds that one had not previously understood. Thus noting the arrival dates of summer migrants in one year tells us little, but do it for twenty years and you will be able to see how weather, for example, influences the northward progress of these birds in the spring. Such discoveries are more likely if you establish a definite project rather than simply collect records at random. Peter Goodfellow's book serves admirably to show how such projects can be set up. Some of the projects are simple. Others are less straightforward and demand more commitment. But all will enable the birdwatcher to get more out of his or her hobby.

Particularly significant discoveries are possible when individuals collaborate and in this respect Britain has led the world. The benefits of collaboration were shown by the bird-ringing scheme, established in 1907, and by the census of all the herons in England and Wales first conducted in 1927. In 1933 the British Trust for Ornithology was born, to develop collaborative surveys and research into birds and their habitats.

Today the Trust runs much more than the ringing scheme and the heronries census. Periodically it surveys the abundance and distribution of individual species (the mute swan in 1990 and the nightjar in 1992, for example), and in 1988–91 an atlas of the distribution of all species summering in Britain and Ireland was compiled, following a similar exercise in 1968–72 and a winter atlas in 1981–84. These surveys tell us where our birds are and how many there are of them. Ringing can not only tell us about how many birds migrate about the world but can also provide valuable insights into how long the birds survive and the causes of death. The Nest Record Scheme produces information about the timing of breeding seasons, how many eggs are laid, breeding success and nest sites. The Common Birds Census and Waterways Birds Survey allow us to register annual changes in national populations. The true potential of all these surveys is now being realized, as the information from all of them is brought together into an integrated programme of population monitoring. This will allow us not only to register changes in populations but also to understand their causes, so we shall be able to distinguish changes that have natural causes from those that may stem from human activity, advising the relevant authorities of the need for conservation action.

These schemes and others allow us to study not only birds but their habitats, to discover not only where birds live and why but also what are the consequences of various management practices on, say, the birds of farmland and woodland. Estuaries are another particularly important habitat for birds in Britain and the Birds of Estuaries Enquiry is a major BTO project; throughout the year dedicated counters brave the British weather to keep tabs on our birds. Such work demands particular expertise and commitment but within the BTO there is something for everyone. A long-running programme of garden bird surveys, for example, enables those whose birdwatching may be confined to ten minutes a day from the window to contribute to our knowledge of familiar birds.

The BTO comprises thousands of members. Some of them contribute just moral support and their membership fees; others contribute hundreds of hours of fieldwork every year. The surveys are co-ordinated by regional representatives, all volunteers, and by staff, who also have the task of making sure that all the information gathered is properly stored and analysed. It is a wonderful collaboration and the major strength of British ornithology. If you want to make it even stronger, please join us.

But why should you? What is the point of it all? What will you get out of it? First, enjoyment. Birdwatching is fun and birdwatching as part of a nationwide team is even more fun, whether it is garden bird recording, nest recording, ringing, or atlasing. Even if you cannot participate in the surveys yourself, joining the Trust allows you to enjoy reading about the work of others in our newsletters and other publications. Secondly, if you do join you are helping to discover more about our birds and the way they live. In these

The gannet is the emblem of the BTO. These two birds were photographed fighting on their breeding ground (see Project 41).

days of increasing human impact on the environment it is essential that we have the hard facts on which to base conservation action. The BTO provides such facts, but can only do so because of the contributions of its members.

The importance of BTO work, especially in relation to conservation, is underlined by the substantial support the Trust gets, via the Joint Nation Conservation Committee (JNCC), from English Nature, the Countryside Council for Wales, and the Nature Conservancy Council for Scotland, as well as from the Department of the Environment (Northern Ireland), the Irish Wildlife Service, the Royal Society for the Protection of Birds (RSPB), and many others. So, use this book to discover ways in which you can expand your birdwatching horizons and join the BTO to make your contributions really count!

Jeremy Greenwood, October 1991

1. GETTING STARTED

*Even as a skilled carpenter can work better with good tools,
so a good birdwatcher needs to be well equipped.*

The three game books of the Earls of Morley, of Saltram House, Devon, are very interesting manuscript notebooks. They record all the gamebirds (birds for the pot), such as pheasants, partridges and wildfowl, which were bagged on the estate. Some entries make harrowing reading for a birdwatcher.

> **ENTRY FROM AN OLD ESTATE NOTEBOOK**
>
> **3rd Nov. 1896 Hardwick Wood**
> 638 pheasants (346 male, 292 female)
> 12 guns. WP Vivien
> 120 pheasants in Catby Meadow
>
> **7th Nov. 1906 Hardwick Wood**
> 860 pheasants. 11 guns
>
> **8th Nov. 1906 Hardwick Wood**
> 601 pheasants
>
> At the end of the 1890–91 season Lord Morley wrote: 'The worst year for partridge for many years. All drowned by the wet weather of June and July. I gave up shooting them early. Pheasants I reared about 1200 – bad year for wild birds. Woodcock very few indeed.'

The Earl's interest in birds and that of a birdwatcher today seem to have little in common. However, the one thing they both have is a notebook. Although the great ornithologists of the 18th and 19th centuries were as quick to shoot and collect specimens as the game-loving country gentlemen, they were also indefatigable in amassing great notebooks and in publishing fine journals. Today, we owe much of our knowledge of birds to the detailed observations and notes of such men as the Reverend Gilbert White who

The grey partridge is still reared for sport, but in many parts of Britain it is a scarce farmland bird.

first differentiated the three Old World 'leaf warblers': willow warbler, wood warbler and chiffchaff.

This meticulous notemaking and that of others at the turn of the century produced a yardstick whereby all other devoted birdwatchers could judge their own studies. The wonder is that although the tireless amateurs who explored the Americas, Africa, the Pacific Islands, Asia and even comparatively well-known Europe, discovered so many birds and so much about them, there is still a vast amount to be learned today.

The value of amateur work today is as great as ever. Clubs and societies for birdwatchers abound and they produce their own magazines and annual reports for counties and other areas. These reports are compiled from the notes of members, and that is where we come in, with a notebook. Whether we are professionals working for the British Trust for Ornithology (BTO), a university or the Ministry of Agriculture, Food and Fisheries, or amateurs spotting for fun, we must have a notebook. We like to think we can remember important things, but few of us can recall with accuracy either the events and sights of a walk a week ago or a holiday a year ago.

The Earls of Morley kept their game-books regularly up-to-date to compare the seasons' shooting and to have a permanent record of the estate's birds, albeit only those that could be shot. Present-day birdwatchers can do no less. If they want their records to stand the test of time and the eagle eye of the editor of their club's annual report, their observations must ring true. It must be very satisfying for an editor if he can quickly judge a record as good because the observer has not only written in great detail but has also dealt with the observations in a logical and generally acceptable way.

The woodcock is a less well-known gamebird that deserves watching all year around. It is an unusual member of the wader family that is found in woods.

The Notebook 1

The observer will be greatly helped if early in his or her note-making career a standard form of entry is adopted.

EXAMPLE FROM A NOTEBOOK

<u>18th FEB</u>. A lovely day. Sunny. Cool but calm, even warm at times.

<u>Cotswold Water Park</u>
A huge series of gravel pits. Many walks. Lake 43 on W side, wonderful collection of wildfowl, several hundred on lake and constant movement overhead to tune of whistling wigeon.
Counted:
c.180 tufted duck
c.70 pochard
a few mallard
c.80 wigeon
at least 10 gadwall
4 goldeneye (1 male)
at least 30 pintail (only 1 male)
1 female teal and a
female <u>SMEW</u>. What a bonus!

SIGNS USED BY BIRDWATCHERS

♀ = female
♂ = male
imm = immature
juv = juvenile
c.70 = approximately 70. 'c.' before any number means 'approximately', but
c/5 = a clutch of five eggs; also c/1, c/3, c/9 etc.

---

and above all the description of the bird itself. When recording an unfamiliar or rare bird a drawing made in the field while you are watching is vital. You, may say 'I can't draw', but with a little practice it is not too difficult with only a few lines to make a reasonable perching bird, duck or wader as shown here.

perching bird

duck

the weather, such as state of tide, flood, lack of water, snow, ice and human disturbance. All can help explain why the birds are there or are perhaps missing compared with an earlier visit.

Unusual records need much more detail about the habitat

In the above example, notice the bold date, locality (each with distinctive underlining), weather and the listing of the birds. Passing on the message that you have heard the first cuckoo of spring, or seen a rare bird, is no good unless you relate it to time and place. Be consistent with your own layout and shorthand. Use a good ball-point pen with black ink (your sketches will look better in black ink than blue) as a pencil can rub out and become illegible. The signs in the panel above are used by all bird-watchers.

Always make a note of any special conditions in addition to

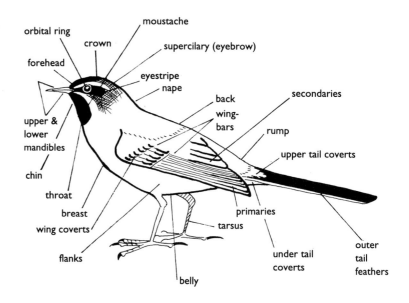

Topography of a bird.

PROJECT 1

wader

Add various remarks around the sketch to fill in the details, as in the page to the right about the rose-coloured starling. A little knowledge of bird anatomy and more particularly a bird's topography (the names of a bird's exterior parts) can assist greatly as shown below.

The vast number of birdwatchers who send in reports today has made it necessary for the recorders of county bird clubs to be very strict about their acceptance of records. The days when a man could say 'I have seen an Osprey; here it is' are thankfully almost gone. Your trophy today must be your notebook record.

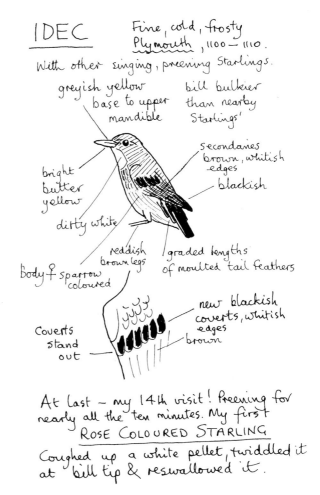

1 DEC — Fine, cold, frosty Plymouth, 1100 – 1110.

With other singing, preening Starlings.

greyish yellow base to upper mandible

bill bulkier than nearby Starlings'

bright butter yellow

dirty white

secondaries brown, whitish edges

blackish

reddish brown legs

graded lengths of moulted tail feathers

Body & sparrow coloured

Coverts stand out

new blackish coverts, whitish edges

brown

At last – my 14th visit! Preening for nearly all the ten minutes. My first ROSE COLOURED STARLING

Coughed up a white pellet, twiddled it at bill tip & reswallowed it.

Copy of field sketch and notes for the sighting of a rose-coloured starling, which is a species on the British Birds *rarities list (see Project 2).*

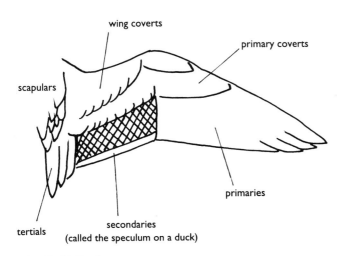

wing coverts

primary coverts

scapulars

primaries

tertials

secondaries
(called the speculum on a duck)

Topography of a bird's wing.

A variety of bird shapes.

The Notebook II

A well-kept notebook is essential if you are going to submit records for a bird report. Later, two developments are possible: writing up a journal and finding a methodical method of storing records (see Project 4).

To assist the busy rarity hunter, the Rarities Committee of *British Birds* magazine has issued a list of birds which they consider each year as British rarities (for a complete list and the address of *British Birds*, *see* pages 124 and 125). Your county recorder will have a local list as well. If you think you have seen any of these birds, write a detailed report. The Rarities Committee's 'Details of an unusual record' form expects you to report under the headings shown in the table below. After submitting an accurate report to your local recorder or the Rarities Committee, the lucky observer will learn that his or her observation has been accepted for publication.

Developing notes into a journal, perhaps illustrated by drawings and some photographs, is a satisfying but time-consuming pastime, with many famous precedents. Perhaps the most famous is Charles Darwin's *A Naturalist's Voyage in HMS Beagle*. A browse through old journals (or diaries) can fill the birdwatcher with nostalgia.

The example to the right reminds us of the virtue of patience in all good birdwatching.

We can all watch birds and be called 'birdwatchers'. Although we may be content to watch sometimes, at other times all we do is look. To 'look' means 'to direct one's sight towards something' according to the *Oxford Shorter English Dictionary*. The word 'watch', however, has a much more demanding meaning which is 'to keep (a person or thing) in view in order to observe any actions, movements or changes that may occur'. We have to make an important decision: are we going to be passive 'birdlookers' or vaguely labelled 'birders', or active 'birdwatchers'?

The true birdwatcher is never satisfied with looking at a bird. Whether sitting comfortably at a dining-room window or hidden in the heather, he or she wants to

---

INFORMATION NEEDED BY THE *BRITISH BIRDS* RARITIES COMMITTEE

species (number, sex, age)
place
date, time and total duration of
    observations; earlier/later dates
    of observations by others if
    known; first/last dates if known
observer's name, address and
    telephone number
observers who claim the record
who found it?
who first identified it?
who is also reporting it, if known?
was it trapped for ringing? (date
    and ringer if known)
if dead, is it preserved and where?
was it photographed? by whom?
optical aids used

distance from observer
previous experience of the species
experience of similar species: (a)
    same day, (b) previously
weather and lighting conditions
direction of flight
period of observation
species present for comparison: (a)
    alongside the bird, (b) nearby
full account, with description and
    sketches, preferably before
    reference to books (if not
    written on the spot, please add
    any notes that were)
is the record 100% certain?
any who disagree?

JOURNAL ENTRY SHOWING THE NEED FOR PATIENCE

14th June 1976
Minsmere, Suffolk

I heard the first grasshopper warbler at 9.30pm. I soon heard a couple more and decided to get as close as possible to one. After a stumbling, crouching approach over ditched rough ground through long heather I stopped maybe twenty yards from one. In the warm-tinted light shed by the almost set sun I found him perched on the low branch of a fir about eighteen inches from the ground and in full view. Its strange song is curious but it was its movements which caught my attention. It walked very slowly and deliberately along the branches, in a horizontal posture, picking for food. Occasionally, when motivated by another male singing some yards away, it stopped and stretched itself up, appearing very slim. With bill raised nearly vertical and white chin shining, it reeled in reply.

PROJECT 2

Very carefully made notes are necessary if you are to convince someone else that you have identified one of the American 'peeps'. This one is a white-rumped sandpiper.

know something about the bird and that involves watching it, patiently. It means taking notes and training oneself to watch carefully. It is not by magic that a birdwatcher identifies a bird. If it seems magic to a novice, it is only a magic which anyone can learn. Binoculars and telescopes (*see* Project 3) are all very well, but only after the eyes have been trained to watch, and the pen has been made to record will the novice birdwatcher begin to improve his or her skills.

A DAY DURING 'THE SIBERIAN FREEZE' OF 1987

<u>17th January</u>

Light easterly breeze, overall high cloud. Almost no birds at breakfast time. I've baited the ground under the cherry with seed for several days: a couple of chaffinches came each day. Where are the rest?

09.55: 6 chaffinches: the best for the week!

10.25: linnet in the cherry, and on the ground beneath 6 chaffinches and a male reed bunting, our first ever. Really handsome, splendidly marked.

10.40: chaffinches up to 10 but no bunting.

12.00: came home to the flock of chaffinches. Put up 18 x 4 feet shelf net. 13.02 caught and ringed a female chaffinch.

14.20/30: marvellous 10 minutes. Firstly, I netted and ringed a female brambling (first winter). Lovely plumage in the hand. Weighed 26g, 2g heavier than a chaffinch a few minutes before. Then I was straight out after releasing that to ring a male firecrest (first winter), second ever ringed in the garden and our sixth record.

14.55: male and female reed buntings have just flown on to the seed! Both feeding busily, in just one place unlike the chaffinches which fidget around. Disturbed by passers-by on the path. Female was so sparrow-like it was only when she flicked her tail and the white outer feathers showed that I realized she was there.

15.00: they're back, with 3 blue tits, 2 great tits and 10 chaffinches. The buntings fed, or rested in the cherry, on and off until 16.15 when they suddenly flew out of the garden down the valley.

22.00: thaw still continuing.

Binoculars and Telescopes

It is fair to say that most birdwatchers find that much of the excitement, joy and satisfaction from birdwatching comes from the enhanced, magnified view that binoculars and telescopes give.

Today, new birdwatchers must accept that this project is going to cost them (or their relatives!) a lot of money, not just time and effort. Regularly, magazines advertise over twenty different binoculars, ranging in price from under £100 to the cost of a second-hand car.

Which model and size is best? *British Birds* and *Bird Watching* magazines publish surveys with helpful comments. Some people will be able to buy the best; others must be more circumspect. Basically, there are three types of binocular on offer: prismatic, roof-prism and compact. The third provides children with binoculars that are of a size and weight that are easy to handle. Price aside, everyone should consider the factors in the panel.

If you handle several binoculars before you buy your own you will be able to judge what sort suits you best. Are you heavy-handed and so need to buy a rubber-armoured pair? Do you wear glasses? You need to beware of some binoculars which give a poor field of view to spectacle wearers?

More and more birdwatchers now own a telescope too. With a magnification of 20x or more (separate eyepieces or zoom can provide up to 60x or 70x) a telescope can reveal wonders, which are far away on a lake, mudflat or distant hillside. Many good telescopes are available which are

easy to handle, give bright images with no fuzziness at the edge of the picture, and focus quickly and surely. However, although some birdwatchers do use their 'scopes on their own, most keep them permanently fixed to a light-weight tripod – an added expense but essential when watching in an exposed position. Although the high magnification of a telescope is its appeal, the higher the magnification the brighter the light that is needed to allow one to see a bright image. So, although a telescope may have a 60x magnification, poor weather would not allow the owner to use it properly. Get used to using binoculars first!

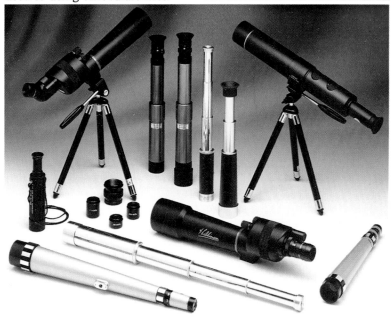

This selection shows traditional and usually cheaper one- or two-draw telescopes and several modern prismatic ones, such as the two on tripods.

Other Equipment

Although this chapter is about getting started, each project actually helps the birdwatcher to keep going. Whatever the binoculars see and the notebook records needs to be stored in some way.

A pile of notebooks is not really useful. The notes need to be extracted and methodically put into categories. This is particularly true of the modern notebook: the miniature tape recorder.

Many naturalists now speak their notes onto a tape that gives thirty minutes of recording. To be useful, that material must be transcribed. The old way would have been to copy it all into a notebook or onto a card index, usually containing dozens of cards. The new way is to put all the information into a personal computer.

The computer can store an incredible number of records, and the user can retrieve the information almost instantly. This database might be a package specially designed for the birdwatcher's machine, which he adapts to his own purposes; or it might be a specially designed birdwatcher's programme. Whichever, he will be able readily to store and retrieve information such as that shown in the panel.

Other programmes for personal computers allow a birdwatcher to be a researcher, by collating records, making statistical calculations and displaying data in graphs and histograms. By printing out the information, such as the example on the right, copies can be passed on to other interested birdwatchers and the editors of county bird reports.

Having a personal computer will encourage the birdwatcher to store records methodically and encourage him to ask questions about his records, which his computer can help solve (*see page 125 for the address of NatureBASE*).

COMPUTER DATABASES FOR THE BIRDWATCHER

- Life list
- Holiday list
- Garden list
- County list
- First and last records each year of migrants
- Record for each species, with special notes for each
- Checklist of bird books
- Ringing list
- Wildfowl counts
- Nestbox scheme information
- Local breeding records

EXAMPLE OF A COMPUTER PRINTOUT

```
BIRDS SEEN IN THE AREA OF HORSHAM MARSH, KENT,
   JUNE 1987 - NOV 1987 AND JULY 1988 - END 1988

species:          Avocet
other details:    6
1st seen:         10/09/88
other sightings:
house or vicinity:        v
breeding evidence:
other:            on Horsham creek

species:          Bunting, reed
other details:    female
1st seen:         20/09/87
other sightings:1987: 1/10. 1988: 4/6, 8/8,
25/9,           22/10 (2)
house or vicinity:        v
breeding evidence:
other:            on Horsham marsh

species:          Chaffinch
other details:
1st seen:         05/06/87
other sightings:Resident. Heard most days in
June.                Infrequent after that.
house or vicinity:        h
breeding evidence:        Singing male
other:
```

2. NESTS

Although a bird's nesting period lasts only a few weeks, that part of its life is especially interesting and is often a new birdwatcher's introduction to the serious study of birds.

For many people, it is a great delight to have birds nesting in their gardens. Even non-birdwatchers enthuse over blue tits in the nest box, the blackbird in the honeysuckle by the back door, and the eggs of the song thrush. They all bring out the protective spirit in everyone in the house, all of whom will be upset if a grey squirrel eats the eggs, or the nest is deserted because the hen bird is caught by the neighbour's cat. Several species are known to nest regularly in gardens, even in towns and cities. Many others breed so secretly that they go about their daily business unnoticed and householders never discover their nests. Thus, suburban shrubberies are transformed into unofficial bird sanctuaries. In contrast, young starlings under the eaves make so much noise that many people try to make sure there are no holes under the roof! Sadly, house martins are not favourites either because they foul walls and windows with mud and droppings. However, a birdwatcher who has a bird nesting in his garden has a golden opportunity to study the species at close quarters.

Although facts abound for many of these common birds, and the details may be read in handbooks, the best way to understand something of the rhythm of a species' breeding cycle is to follow the fortunes of a pair that can be closely studied. One day, these observations may stand the apprentice birdwatcher in good stead because, although birdwatching is a favourite pastime in the Western World, in many places hundreds of the known species of birds still have not revealed the secrets of their nests. Today's

BIRDS WHICH REGULARLY BREED IN THE CITY AND TOWN	
Woodpigeon	Great tit
Collared dove	Blue tit
Starling	Chaffinch
Blackbird	Greenfinch
Mistle thrush	Dunnock
Song thrush	Wren
Robin	Kestrel
Carrion crow	House sparrow
Magpie	Tawny owl
Jackdaw	Pied wagtail
Rook	Goldcrest

garden-watcher may be tomorrow's traveller who discovers the first known nest of either the chocolate tyrant of Patagonia, the uluguru shrike of Tanzania or the green-backed honeyeater of New Guinea and northern Australia.

The many interesting studies which can be made in the garden, wood or on farmland place a great responsibility on each watcher. The welfare of the birds must be considered paramount. If a bird shows anxiety, the observer must move away as he may be keeping the bird from either incubating its eggs or brooding its young. Some species, such as the jay and yellowhammer, are easily made to desert their nests. Ideal views of breeding birds can be had by watching at a safe distance with binoculars *(see also* Project 7).

In the United Kingdom the Wildlife and Countryside Act, 1981, is of great importance to anyone

GENERAL LIST OF SCHEDULE 1 SPECIES

Crossbill
Owl, barn (England & Wales)
Quail
Kingfisher
Plover, little ringed
Redstart, black

SPECIAL LIST OF SCHEDULE 1 SPECIES

Avocet
Bee-eater
Bittern
Bittern, little
Bluethroat
Brambling
Bunting, cirl
Bunting, Lapland
Bunting, snow
Buzzard, honey
Chough
Corncrake
Crake, spotted
Curlew, stone
Diver, black-throated
Diver, great northern
Diver, red-throated
Dotterel
Duck, long-tailed

Eagle, golden
Eagle, white-tailed
Falcon, gyr
Fieldfare
Firecrest
Garganey
Goldeneye
Godwit, black-tailed
Goose, greylag
Goshawk
Grebe, black-necked
Grebe, Slavonian
Greenshank
Gull, little
Gull, Mediterranean
Harrier (all species)
Heron, purple
Hobby
Hoopoe
Kite, red
Merlin
Oriole, golden
Osprey
Owl, barn (Scotland)
Owl, snowy
Peregrine
Phalarope, red-necked
Pintail
Plover, Kentish
Redwing
Rosefinch, scarlet
Ruff
Sandpiper, green

Sandpiper, purple
Sandpiper, wood
Scaup
Scoter, common
Scoter, velvet
Serin
Shorelark
Shrike, red-backed
Spoonbill
Stilt, black-winged
Stint, Temminck's
Storm-petrel, Leach's
Swan, Bewick's
Swan, whooper
Tern, black
Tern, little
Tern, roseate
Tit, bearded
Tit, crested
Treecreeper, short-toed
Warbler, Cetti's
Warbler, Dartford
Warbler, marsh
Warbler, Savi's
Whimbrel
Woodlark
Wryneck

N.B. A rarer breeding species than these may be added to the Special List without warning, so if you find one, contact the BTO's Licensing Officer for clearance.

connected with the study of nesting birds. All British species are protected while breeding, and the rarest, and several declining species, are especially protected (see above). Anyone who wilfully disturbs any wild bird in the First Schedule while it is on or near a nest containing eggs or young, is liable to a very heavy fine.

A Nature Conservancy Council permit to allow birdwatchers to study any of these species at or near the nest may be sought from the BTO (for address *see* page 125; *see also* Project 56, Photographing Birds). The species likely to be studied in the garden or during visits to the countryside are not on the special list, but nevertheless great care must be taken not to upset any birds.

The chaffinch is one of Britain's commonest and prettiest birds. Here a male is bringing food to young at the nest.

Nestboxes 1

A bird that nests in a nestbox gives great pleasure to the bird-lover, and provides a birdwatcher with a controlled situation for study purposes.

Tits are most often the tenants in Britain; in North America purple martins nest in colonies and 100 or more may nest in specially erected bird houses.

The sizes of the box are approximate; there is no need to be too fussy. The beauty of this project is that it uses up scrap wood. Seasoned hardwood lasts best.

In North America the purple martin nests in artificial 'high-rise flats'. Each bird house is made from a hollow gourd. Over 100 birds may nest in one colony.

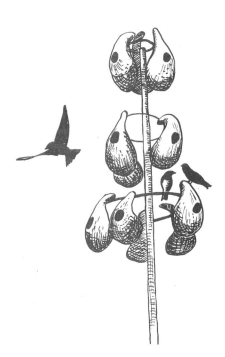

The photograph opposite shows a typical nestbox for great, blue and coal tits in Britain, and crested tits in Europe. Many European starlings, house sparrows, tree sparrows and pied flycatchers will use boxes like this if the entrance hole is a little larger, 4 to 5cm in diameter. Open-fronted boxes attract robins, spotted flycatchers and pied wagtails.

Plywood is not suitable. Do not treat the wood with preservatives. If the box is going up in your garden make sure it cannot be reached by a cat, and does not have the sun shining on it in the heat of the day: north facing on a tree trunk or garage or garden wall is fine. There is no need to provide a perch on the box, but perches nearby in shrubbery or trees will give the birds a safe route to the box.

Make sure when the box is made that the hinge and catch enable you to lift the lid smoothly. Lower and shut it slowly and carefully, as tits and pied flycatchers will sit tight, bold tits will hiss at you! If the bird is sitting, do not be tempted to flush it to see the eggs. Careful watching will show you when the hen leaves, thus providing you with a safe time to view the clutch or young.

After the nest has been used, and all the young have flown, the

PIED FLYCATCHERS IN BOXES

In Britain, the pied flycatcher breeds almost exclusively in upland deciduous woods. It can readily be tempted into nestboxes instead of a natural hole. It nests in loose colonies and great success has been had in North Wales, Herefordshire and Devon in attracting this lovely bird to breed. In Devon, before 1950, it bred sporadically. In 1955, at the National Nature Reserve, Yarner Wood, pied flycatchers first bred in boxes, and they have done ever since. Several other sites now have flourishing colonies and ringing has shown that birds from different colonies interbreed with one another. Now over 200 pairs nest in Devon. There can be no doubt that the breeding range of this species has been extended by its use of thoughtfully and hopefully placed boxes. Detailed, scientific studies have been made – and sometimes spoilt as one Devon colony has become a favourite home of dormice!

box should be cleaned out so that no nest parasites are left there to breed. If permission has been obtained from a landowner to erect several boxes in a wood, all the boxes at the end of the season must be checked, not just the successful ones. Droppings must be cleaned from roost boxes, incomplete nests cleared away and wasps' nests removed. Boxes in poor repair must be mended or replaced.

In some gardens and woods, boxes must be protected from predators: woodpeckers will drill through the front of a box to get at young; grey squirrels will enlarge the hole. A metal plate can help prevent this. Boxes made of a cement and sawdust mix are squirrel-proof. In other areas, boxes can be dangled from a branch on a strong wire to prevent weasels raiding the nest. A cone of plastic over the roof of a hanging nest box prevents mammals trying to climb down.

*Typical tit nestbox in a garden (**right**), which can be constructed from a single plank (**below**).*

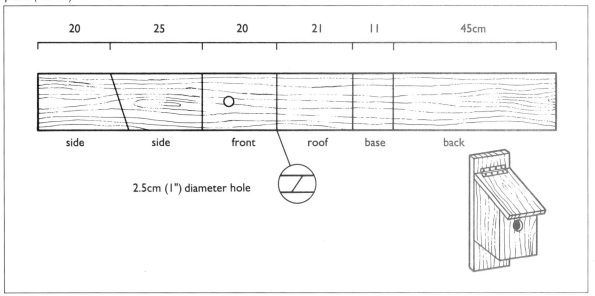

20	25	20	21	11	45cm

| side | side | front | roof | base | back |

2.5cm (1") diameter hole

Nestboxes II

A nestbox need not be the conventional box, as seen in Project 5. It can be anything constructed with the specific purpose of attracting birds to nest.

Conservation of endangered species can be actively helped by the erection of boxes, so this project is recommended to county naturalist and conservation trusts.

Raptors (hawks and falcons) and owls especially need to be looked after. They are at the end of the food chain and their populations are in most danger from pesticide pollution and habitat destruction. The barn owl has greatly decreased in numbers in recent years when it has been poisoned by pesticides, killed on the roads, drowned in farm troughs, and lost nest sites through trees in hedges being destroyed (with the owls' nesthole) and barns being converted to make cottage homes. This is not so much a project for a hopeful individual, but one for a dedicated, licensed team, such as The Barn Owl Trust in Devon and The Hawk and Owl Trust in Lincolnshire, which could often

do with extra funds and pairs of hands to help (for addresses *see* page 125).

Every year, thousands of buildings are re-roofed. Swifts are particularly attracted to old, pantiled roofs (the 's' shape of pantiles often gave swifts enough space at the eaves to wriggle into the roof space). In the Western Palaearctic hardly any swifts nest in natural sites in holes in trees or cliffs. So, as old roofs are modernized, nest sites are destroyed. A new and, it is hoped, on-going

SPECIALITY NESTBOXES

- Imitation riverbank tunnels for kingfishers.

- Imitation rabbit burrows for wheatears on downland.

- Artificial islands for common terns (such as those at Abbotsbury and Attenborough Reserve, Nottingham).

- Predator-proof platforms for ringed plovers or terns.

- Rooftop platform for white storks (in the Netherlands).

- Platform on a pole for ospreys (in North America and Scotland).

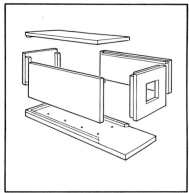

Construction of a barn owl nestbox. The entrance hole should be no smaller than 15cm (6in) square and must have a perching platform in front.

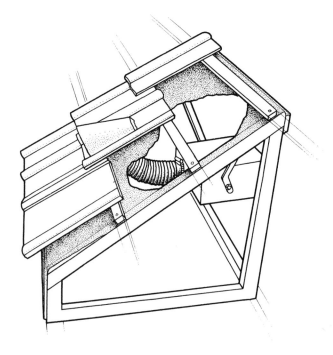

Design of a swift nestbox incorporating the special swift nest-tile, as used by Operation Swift in the east of England. The nest box measures 30 x 30 x 15cm (12 x 12 x 6 inches) and has a lift-up door to allow access. In the Netherlands, special boxes have been screwed to the soffits under the gutter.

PROJECT 6

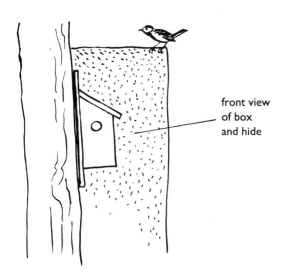

front view
of box
and hide

Artificial nests for house martins beneath the eaves.

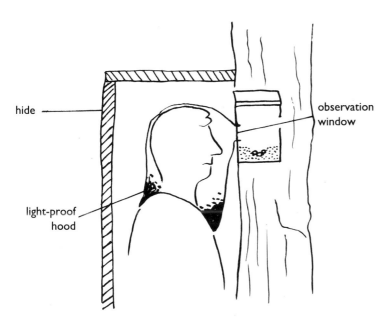

hide

observation window

light-proof hood

A birdwatcher can look right into a nestbox if a hide is placed right up against the nestbox, one side of which is made of clear perspex.

project encourages householders, councils and housing associations to incorporate a swift nest-tile and nestbox in a new roof. If you think you can help, contact Operation Swift (for address *see* page 125).

An unusual observation nestbox was used by Edward A. Armstrong to study wrens at work inside their box. This could be adapted and used in the study of several other species (*see* other Projects in the rest of this chapter, and Chapters 4 and 5). With care, it is amazing how closely one can watch breeding birds and make detailed notes of, for

instance, the behaviour of the adults, feeding rates, food, and behaviour of the young.

If you want something novel, boxes for house martins are ideal, provided that you have overhanging eaves high enough to simulate an overhang on a cliff (a house martin's natural nest site, such as they still use on a sea-cliff at Tintagel, Cornwall, and the limestone cliff, Malham Tarn, in the Yorkshire Dales). Such boxes are advertised in bird magazines. If you like working with clay or papier maché (or even cement), they can be made on a wire frame; make several because house martins are colonial, and though large colonies are rare, small numbers together are common. They will even settle in new housing estates. Make sure that a ready supply of mud is nearby in spring so that they can renovate nests, or even build a new one beside your box.

Many birds will readily take to nestboxes where nest sites are scarce, such as in gardens, open farmland with few trees, plantations and coppiced woodland. The BTO Guide No. 20, *Nestboxes* by Chris du Feu will help you make a nest site for many birds, from mute swan to robin.

PROJECT 7

Studying a Nesting Bird

As the details of the daily lives of nesting birds are written in the observer's notebook, the breeding biology of the species under study will slowly come to light.

It is imperative that a birdwatcher who intends to study the nesting birds of a defined area, or one particular species, follows a code of conduct that will put the birds first and respect the law.

CODE OF CONDUCT

- Keep each visit brief.
- Go out prepared – with notebook and nest record cards (see Project 9).
- Take a mirror on a stick to look into high nests.
- Take care while searching.
- Cover your tracks when leaving.
- Do not inspect a nest if a predator is nearby.
- Do not go, or carry on, nest-hunting in the rain.

Most observations can be made at a distance; when the nest has to be looked at closely, do it quickly when the adult birds are away, if possible. Topics 8, 9 and 10 in the panel above right could best be studied from a hide (see Project 52). If a nestbox is in use, lift the inspection cover slowly, look in and, as soon as possible, carefully close the box again if the hen is incubating or brooding; do not flush the sitting bird. A detailed examination of the nests themselves can be made in late summer or early autumn when it is certain that they are no longer in use.

The close examination of a nest is thrilling. For example, one long-tailed tit's nest I analysed from a wood by a creek some years ago was lined with 1,601 feathers, ranging from about 0.8cm to 9cm (0.25 –3.5in) long (the bird is only 14cm or 5.5in long). The feathers were woodpigeon mostly, but also from blackbird, robin, song thrush, house sparrow, chaffinch, tawny owl, mallard, curlew and farmyard chicken. Other nests have less than 1,000 feathers, but over 2,000 have been recorded (see Project 54 about feather collections).

No one should ever think of making an exhibition of birds' nests unless the nests are collected in late autumn when one can be sure that they are not in use.

TEN NESTING STUDIES

1. Description of nests and nest sites.
2. Length of building time.
3. Comparative rôle of male and female in nest building.
4. Date of laying first egg and each subsequent egg.
5. Clutch size, i.e. total number of eggs laid.
6. Incubation period, i.e. length of time from beginning of brooding to hatching.
7. Fledging period, i.e. length of time before young fly.
8. Feeding rates of the young: different days compared; different times of day compared.
9. Comparison of help provided by cock and hen (and even young of an earlier brood, e.g. moorhen).
10. Length of the breeding season.

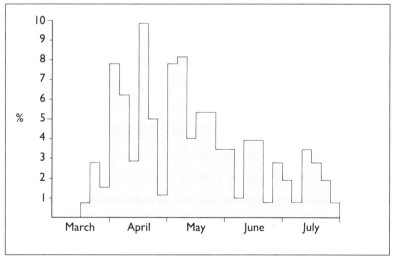

The breeding season of the song thrush in the Oxford area, showing the percentages of clutches that were started in each five-day period. The data were collected from the study of 145 nests (from Mayer-Gross, 1964).

24

Special Nests

A nestwatcher can compile a fascinating collection of facts about unusual nests and nest sites. An unusual nest could be a normal one in a strange site, or one made of unusual materials.

Many birdwatchers who live in country districts where birds such as skylarks, pipits, plovers, partridges and other ground-nesters breed, have little chance of providing nest sites for them like the nestbox-watcher can for woodland species. However, they have the opportunity of protecting existing nests from the heavy feet of cattle or sheep. In 1964, Hendriksma described and illustrated wire protectors for lapwings' and black-tailed godwits' nests which he had used in the Netherlands. Up to 70 per cent of nests had been lost in the area by being crushed by cattle; after protection this was reduced to 7.5 per cent. The barbed-wire frame must be at least 60cm (2 feet) tall to enable the bird to enter the cage (*see* below). A wireless version of a squatter shape has been successful too.

Garden nests can be protected from predators by putting a wire-mesh cage around the nest, improvising the shape according to the nest's position. Blackbirds and song thrushes are quite tolerant of such disturbance. Care must be taken to ensure the mesh is big enough for the nesting birds to pass through (about 7cm or 2.75 in). If you are monitoring a protected nest for the BTO's Nest Record Scheme, you must describe the protection on the nest record card.

Isolated observations could develop into one of the following projects:

1. What proportion of unusual nests is in a given population?
2. What species are more prone to nest atypically?
3. Is the use of unusual materials fortuitous or dependent on a noticeable source of supply?
4. Are the unusual sites a result of population pressures and a consequent shortage of normal positions?
5. What are the reactions of one species to another nesting very close by?

On the last point I have seen a song thrush's nest just below a long-tailed tit's nest in a gorse bush, and a grey wagtail nesting less than a metre from a dipper.

Regular and repeated recording of such eccentricities can be interesting in its own right, and can also help train the observer to improve his watching and recording techniques.

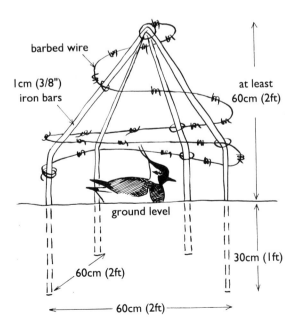

barbed wire

1cm (3/8")
iron bars

at least 60cm (2ft)

ground level

60cm (2ft)

30cm (1ft)

60cm (2ft)

A wire cage used to protect a lapwing's nest from cattle. If the cage is placed near the nest and moved closer gradually, it will get the bird used to the protection instead of being scared by it. A similar design to a smaller scale would protect a skylark's nest.

The Nest Record Scheme

The BTO's Nest Record Scheme is over fifty years old, and is the largest scheme of its kind in the world.

You do not need to be a member of the BTO to take part in the scheme. They will be delighted to receive your records of actively used nests from all habitats, from seashore to mountain top, from garden to forest. Each nest should be visited preferably more than once, and should be carefully recorded on one card with full details of each visit and the nesting habitat, as shown in the example.

To date, over three-quarters of a million cards are held by the BTO; over 30,000 new ones are received annually from over 1,000 nest-watchers. Offers from new recorders are much appreciated. There is plenty of scope for urban and suburban birdwatchers to help; you do not have to

make difficult expeditions to join in. Help from under-represented areas (Ireland, southern and eastern Scotland) and with regard to under-recorded species would be specially welcomed (for BTO address *see* page 125).

Each year, the nest record cards are filed. Much of the data is computerized and analyses are made for many species of:
1. laying period;
2. clutch sizes;
3. incubation, hatching, nestling, fledging periods;
4. breeding success, i.e. the proportion of nests started from which young are reared;
5. nest sites and breeding habitats.

Thanks to computerization in 1988, the BTO is able now to

BTO'S LIST OF MONITORED COMMON SPECIES

Mute swan	Song thrush
Sparrowhawk	Sedge warbler
Buzzard	Reed warbler
Kestrel	Whitethroat
Moorhen	Blackcap
Ringed plover	Wood warbler
Lapwing	
Stock dove	Willow warbler
Collared dove	
Tawny owl	Spotted flycatcher
Skylark	Nuthatch
Swallow	
Meadow pipit	Magpie
Pied wagtail	Raven
Wren	Starling
Dunnock	Chaffinch
Robin	Linnet
Redstart	Yellowhammer
Wheatear	Reed bunting

TEN UNDER-RECORDED SPECIES IN THE NEST RECORD SCHEME

Species	Total cards received to end of 1990	Number received in:			
		1987	1988	1989	1990
Shelduck*	217	10	0	8	8
Tufted duck	853	56	53	45	25
Puffin*	165	0	0	0	0
Turtle dove	1,731	31	20	23	37
Swift*	953	28	36	50	34
Green woodpecker	266	7	13	13	9
Yellow wagtail*	857	13	28	17	18
Willow tit	382	15	19	9	11
Jay	1,261	34	44	34	50
Goldfinch	2,591	49	47	74	65

Those species marked with an asterisk have each had a book written about them (see Project 54), yet there is still more we could discover. Here is a really challenging project!

TOP TEN RECORDED SPECIES UP TO AND INCLUDING 1989

Species	Number of cards
Blackbird	111,006
Song thrush	65,613
Blue tit	46,597
Swallow	33,911
Great tit	29,748
Dunnock	26,601
Linnet	22,799
Pied flycatcher	19,265
Woodpigeon	17,885
Chaffinch	17,256

Ringed plover nest with three eggs, beautifully camouflaged on a shingle shore. This species can be found nesting on suitable shores all around Britain.

monitor every year the laying dates and clutch sizes of at least twenty-seven species, which have been carefully chosen to represent all types of birds, and birds from a wide range of habitats and life-styles.

Already, statistically significant differences have been found in the laying dates and clutch sizes of some species compared with previous years, and one is forced to wonder why. All this information can be used to help conservation work in the United Kingdom and Ireland (which are often thought of as a unit in zoological terms). Since the scheme started, over 100 papers and books have been published using data from the cards.

In addition to the top ten species shown in the panel above, moorhen, lapwing, robin, willow warbler, wren, starling, house sparrow, tree sparrow and greenfinch also have five-figure card collections. The BTO welcomes more information on these species: this is the only way to keep

track of these populations from year to year. The Nest Record Scheme and many other research and conservation projects are reviewed and the results published annually by the BTO in *Britain's Birds: The Conservation and Monitoring Review*, the first of which was published in 1991.

Long-tailed tit with a nest-lining feather.

Species						County/Region			19		BTO Ref.

A BTO nest record card. The reverse of the card is divided into two. The observer has to mark special boxes to show the habitat surrounding the nesting area, and details of the nest site. The card has been specially designed to aid computer analysis of the data.

3. SONG

Much of the excitement of birdwatching is actually to be found in listening to birds. A birdwatcher who does not learn to listen is only half a birdwatcher!

Primitive man certainly hunted, and even worshipped, birds. His cave paintings attest to this. One aspect of birds' lives which seems to have appealed greatly is their song. Stone Age whistles made of bone have been found and they suggest that thousands of years ago men tried to imitate bird calls and songs. Man's earliest writings tell of birds singing, especially the excitement of hearing springtime songs after the cold and wet of winter. One of the oldest references is in an old Hebrew love poem in the Bible, written about 200BC:

My beloved speaks and says to me:
'Arise my love, my fair one, and come away;
for lo, the winter is past, the rain is over and gone.
The flowers appear on the earth,
the time of singing has come,
and the voice of the turtledove is heard in our land'.

The Song of Solomon, ch. 2,
vv 10–12

Traditionally, in western Europe, the bird song extolled above all others is the nightingale's. It is one of the main contestants in the medieval poetic dialogues from the 13th century, *The Owl and the Nightingale* and *The Thrush and the Nightingale*; and an early 14th century manuscript has a lyric beginning 'when the nyhtegale singes the wodes waxen greene'. The persistent, metronomic two notes of the cuckoo were heralding the summer for farming men long before an anonymous minstrel wrote in 1225:

Sumer is icumen in
Llude sing cuccu
Groweth sed and bloweth med
And springth the wde nu
Sing cuccu!

In more recent times musicians and biologists have listened carefully and have tried to copy or explain the sounds they hear. Both have largely failed. Yet the fascination still persists. Birdwatchers today are still coming to grips with understanding bird vocalizations. With so much noise pollution about us, we should

---

FIND THIS BIRD SONG!

Bullfinch: unlike many finches it has no song as we usually think of it, just a low, faint, broken warble, audible only at close range.

Snipe: by marsh or moor, a sound like goat or sheep bleating above your head will be this bird's song, produced by air rushing over extended outer tail feathers.

Spotted flycatcher: high-pitched notes, hardly worthy of being called song; sounds like a squeaky gate hinge, often going on for minutes on end from a high perch.

Goldcrest: extremely high-pitched, thin repetition of one note, ending on a flourish; inaudible to many listeners even at close range.

Reed bunting: its three or four notes, *tweek-tweek-tirrik*, monotonously repeated could easily be passed by and not heard as a song.

endeavour to keep our ears in training by making the effort to find the little natural sounds, and to 'listen in perspective'. Even as the eye picks up visual images from foreground to background, so the ear can listen in depth, if the listener makes a conscious effort. Over-dependence on radio, record-player, walkman – all foreground noises – dulls the aural perception of many people. Perhaps careful attention to the projects in this chapter will redress the situation and help to people the countryside with a few more Dr Dolittles.

Before we start on the proper projects, here is a simple challenge: find and listen to the song of a species that many people have never or rarely heard, although the bird itself is not uncommon (see panel for suggested target list).

In 1896, R. Bowdler Sharpe, who was a much respected ornithologist and lecturer working at the British Museum, published a book called *Wonders of the Bird World*. Not one of its thirteen chapters dealt with bird song. The modern scientific study of bird vocalizations has progressed a long way since then but, nevertheless, my bookshelves have hardly anything on the topic compared with the many books about the birds of geographical areas, the monographs (i.e. one volume on the life of one species), titles on migration and behaviour, and field guides. It is hard to write a book about sounds (as we shall see in Project 13). Yet birdwatchers still find that the nightingale's rich melodious warbling and powerful crescendo stir deep feelings, and the cuckoo calls our attention to spring (although BTO Guide 15, *Early and Late Dates for Summer Migrants*, accepts only sight records for the 'first cuckoo of spring' for fear of including hoaxes by skilful imitators!). The song of the nightingale, once heard, is so powerful and creative that a listener cannot help but recognize it; the cuckoo's song is impossible to confuse with any other bird's. Most bird songs are not so easy, as we shall see.

To ignore the calls and songs of birds is to ignore a world of wonder, beauty and fun. Every journey can be enriched by careful listening; every stop by a pool, seashore or woodland glade cannot only be a thrill of movement and colour, but also of sounds, be they the tiny warblings of a treecreeper or the ear-aching roar of hundreds of alarmed great black-backed gulls disturbed from their island roost. Perhaps, like me, you will find one sound which again and again sends a strange, indefinable feeling through you: a peregrine's call, swifts screaming, a woodlark high above, wild geese migrating, or as John Masefield put it:

What would improve such beauty, nay what could?
My great friend said, 'Some birds might ... curlews
    would.'
And at her word a cry of curlews came,
Crying their cry of creatures never tame ...

The blackbird, like many songbirds, chooses a prominent position from which to proclaim in song its territory and advertise for a mate.

Recognizing Bird Songs

One of the most difficult projects a birdwatcher can undertake is learning to recognize bird calls, yet in a way it is one of the most important.

Some people have no ear for sounds and have difficulty in distinguishing tunes, let alone slightly varying notes, but if one can make the effort to identify each sound, the ears can reveal an amazing number of birds which the eyes fail to spot.

I am always grateful that I had a good teacher when I was only ten. Certainly the easiest and best way to learn is to go about with a skilled bird-listener, because the listener's ear starts to tune in with the teacher's and, quickly, the worth of listening as well as watching becomes obvious. A trip may reveal thirty species by sight alone; the same trip may record double that number if the observer is following up sounds. I have led field meetings at which members have been most excited by the numbers of contacts made with birds on the strength of identifying them by sound alone. As the observer gains in experience a record may be valid solely on the strength of a call heard as, for example, in any census work (*see* Chapter 6).

STRANGE SONGS

Capercaillie: begins with clicks, getting quicker, followed by a pop like a cork from a bottle, and finally a knife-grinding sound!

Fulmar: guttural, barking notes, *urg-urg-urg* repeated as a cackle.

Grasshopper warbler: rapid trill, sustained, for up to two minutes; sounding mechanical like a sewing machine or angler's reel.

Great spotted woodpecker: both sexes produce a loud sound called 'drumming' by rapidly and repeatedly hitting a dead branch with their bills.

Herring gull: the male points his bill to the sky and gives the 'long call', a loud, trumpeting *kyow-kyow-kyow*.

Pheasant: a loud, crowing *karrk karrk* is followed by a startling whirring of the wings.

Tawny owl: the traditional idea of the tawny owl's song, *to whit-to whoo* is really the call note *to-whit* (or *kewick*) of male or female, plus the song which is actually a prolonged *hoo-hoo* (pause) *oo* (pause) *hooooooo*. In the wild the two are not usually muddled.

The sound of the pheasant's whirring wings are part of its courtship display.

A Species' Vocabulary

By using our voices in different ways, we can signal to the listener particular messages. So, too, a bird uses many different calls to warn or attract.

Birds' vocal utterances are often lumped together as 'calls' or 'songs'. However, they need to be labelled more precisely. Just as our speech can be divided into questions, commands, statements and exclamations, so a bird's vocal communication can be described more precisely, as shown below.

Some bird calls are difficult to assign to a particular category. The call note may be bold and the song simple in structure, as it is in the nuthatch, so there seems little difference to the untrained ear. Other species' calls, such as the great tit's, are hard to analyse simply because they have such a large vocabulary (in 1961 Terry Gompertz published her discovery that the great tit may have at least eighteen types of call, while it was noted that an individual male had at least thirty-two different utterances).

This project – learning the messages in each sound – is essential before more subtle tasks can be tackled such as those explained in Projects 16 and 17. In an article in *New Scientist* in 1981, Dr Clive Catchpole of London University asked the

The great tit's simple two-note song is often written down as teacher, teacher, teacher.

question 'Why do birds sing?' When you have learned to recognize many songs and have started work on Project 15, 40 or 48, you will feel as Dr Catchpole and many other ornithologists do that the first question may have been answered. But there are other questions, such as 'Why are their songs so elaborate?' Go to it. Start listening!

A BIRD'S VOCALIZATIONS

Song: normally a prolonged series of notes, often (to the human ear) melodiously arranged as it is, for example, in the thrush family and many Old World warblers. It is usually a bold sound, often from a prominent position, to proclaim the male's territory or to attract a mate.

Call note: a simple sound to indicate sex, species, locality or the activity engaged in.

Contact note: important to flocking birds that migrate by night (such as the redwings, which in Britain are often first spotted in early October by their plaintive *tseew* calls overhead as the flock endeavours to keep together in the dark, but spaced well enough to avoid collisions). The contact note is also important to birds that flock in winter and feed together (such as waders), and to birds that live in woodland (such as long-tailed tits) and need a call to keep the flock or family in touch.

Alarm note: vital to a bird's survival and usually loud, short and sharp. It has an urgency noticeable even to man. Some birds have several different alarms. For example, a disturbed blackbird may give a rapid burst of calls if flushed by an intruder; it may quietly cluck if anxious rather than alarmed; it will loudly yell ringing staccato note after note when mobbing an owl. Some alarms, such as the last mentioned, are understood by other species. Swallows and starlings have distinctive alarms when harassing a hawk or falcon.

Scientists have recently discovered that flapping of the wings by a male starling while it sings is a signal to attract a mate. Once mated, it just sings and does not flap its wings.

Where Do Birds Sing?

You may think that the songbirds in your garden choose to sing at random. Careful observation will show that this is not so.

Cock birds which sing to proclaim that they have established territories will do so around these territories, regularly using favourite song posts. The local starling may use a chimney pot, the collared dove the pine at the bottom of the garden, and the blackbird often sits on the television aerial.

Hulme has recorded the perches used daily by nine species during the year on a suburban two-mile route in Derbyshire. His results are shown below for eight species using song posts on buildings. These compare with 1,008 natural song posts (trees and branches) and the results would be worth comparing with other parts of the country. Do your wrens sing exclusively on natural song posts? Is the starling the species in your district which uses building song posts most?

How regularly are television aerials used nowadays?

Working in the suburbs is relatively easy. Studying in a wood is not so straightforward. However, if the observer works methodically through the wood, retracing his steps for each visit, and then records all the singing birds on a large scale map, analysis of the records is possible (*see also* Projects 48 and 49). It would be wise to concentrate at first on one species and perhaps, to start with, those that sing within the boundary of a transect you choose to walk each time you visit. A transect is a line across a given habitat which is followed on each study-visit; it would be wise to limit its width to 10m (11 yds) each side of your path. An analysis of a chaffinch showed clearly that the cock not only sang all over its territory, but also it had

favourite trees or bushes from which to sing.

The greenfinch has a rather dull song based on its twittering flight call and the male's characteristic loud, drawn out, nasal *tsweee*. However, it is often excitingly performed in a song flight. Many people think that only skylarks sing in flight, but the greenfinch's strange, erratic circlings are even more arrestingly interesting. The bird looks bat-like as it flies with exaggerated slow wing-beats. It would be interesting to map the flight patterns of particular males to see if there is any regularity in them, comparable say to a chaffinch using a particular song perch.

What other birds regularly sing in flight? You should be able to discover at least six other species.

Very few birds sing from the ground. A study of one which does might be revealing. Many ground-nesting birds, such as the skylark, sing in flight but even one which does not (the wheatear) uses a perch like a wall or boulder.

SONG-POSTS IN SUBURBIA

Perch	Wood-pigeon	Mistle thrush	Song thrush	Blackbird	Robin	Dunnock	Starling	Chaffinch
Gable-end ridge tile	–	1	15	99	1	24	33	9
Other ridge tiles	–	–	2	7	–	6	8	2
Hip ridge tile	–	–	–	3	–	7	–	–
Edge of roof	–	–	–	–	1	–	1	–
Chimney pot	2	–	4	10	–	–	393	–
Chimney stack	–	–	2	11	–	–	27	–
Gutter	–	–	1	10	–	–	19	–
Soil pipe	–	–	–	–	–	–	4	–
Television aerial	–	–	–	15	–	–	11	–
Weathercock	–	–	–	1	–	–	–	–

Recording Bird Song I

The lyrics and tune of a song can be written down as words and notes of music. But how do you write down a garden warbler's warble?

As more bird calls and songs are learned, occasions will arise when the observer will want to record in his notebook what he has heard, so that he can check his findings with a textbook or recording. If a rare bird has been seen and heard, both appearance and sounds must be noted to present a valid record to the local bird club. Bird vocalizations are notoriously difficult to put on paper. No agreed system exists. The editors of *The Birds of the Western Palaearctic*, Vol. V (1988) wrote:

'Exceptionally complex and difficult problems are met in attempting to develop a scientific method of describing and interpreting the vocal utterances of birds ... Phonetic, or onomatopoeic, representation is beset by pitfalls on account of its subjective nature; no major studies have been made of the phonetic content of bird sounds.'

Notations are usually simple, personal transliterations of such well-known calls as *caw, caw, cuckoo, cuckoo* and *chiff-chaff-chiff-chiff-chaff* (but the Dutch write *tjiftjaf* and the Germans *zilpzalp*!). Fluty notes are rendered by 'oo' sounds, metallic notes by hard consonants, and churrs and trills by the repeated letter 'r'. But these take no account of the speed or pitch of the utterance.

Many scientists have attempted to record bird song on the musical staff, using the musical signs. One of the most detailed attempts recently is that of David Hindley, former head of music at Homerton College, Cambridge. He is convinced that much bird song *is* music. He has slowed down the recorded songs of the woodlark, skylark, chaffinch and nightingale so that the human ear can pick out each note (a skylark can sing 230 notes in a second), and has found musical parallels with Bach and Beethoven. If you are musical and have had some training, what songs can you transfer to music manuscript?

A great many calls are not easily tied to a set key or staff notation. Recent attempts to regularize bird-song recording on paper have been rather complicated. A simpler method, perhaps less scientific but easier to remember – which, if followed would be important in standardizing the observer's own notes, allowing valuable comparisons to be made – has been suggested:

Pitch is represented by the vowels i, e, a and o, giving four descending degrees of pitch in that particular bird's compass.

An accent is put over a stressed call. Speed is shown by the way the separate notes are connected:

1. Definitely disjointed notes are separated by a comma: *penk, penk, penk* (a chaffinch call).
2. Notes produced at the rate of about one per second are written separately: *chip chep chip chip chep* (chiffchaff).
3. Notes produced at the rate of about two per second are hyphenated: *twi-twi-twe-twe-twa-twa* (willow warbler).
4. Notes produced at the rate of about four per second are double-hyphenated: *twe--twe--twe--twee--twe* (nuthatch).
5. A very fast series of notes is shown by a trill: *trrrrr* (a quick rattle in a wren's song).

Tone is represented by the consonants which begin the syllables. These vary between 'w' or 'l' for soft tones, through 'tw' to 'ch' for harsh utterances. The exact use of these depends on how the tone strikes the hearer. As examples of the system in action there follow two chaffinch songs:
1.*chip-chip-chí, trrrr tó-si--si--chó.*
2.*twi-twi-twi-twi-twe-twe-twe cha--cha--cha--cha--cha--cha--chí, sa-wía.*

Suffice it to say that once an observer starts recognizing songs and calls he will sooner or later have somehow to write down what he hears.

Song of a bullfinch which was heard singing in April. There is some evidence that each bullfinch has its own individual song.

Recording Bird Song II

Undoubtedly the surest way to record accurately all bird sounds, be they vocal like the nightingale's or mechanical like the snipe's, is to tape-record them.

TAPE RECORDERS

In recent years, the battery-powered transistor tape-recorder has given the birdwatcher an accurate recording tool which is quite easily portable, unlike the equipment of pioneer Ludvig Koch. This was very heavy, very cumbersome and recorded on discs: his sound-book *Songs of Birds* was indeed a labour of love. It is tempting to think that recording bird songs and calls is easy, simply a matter of putting a microphone near a calling bird. But this is far from the truth. A great deal of planning and patience is needed, apart from expense. The easily portable and relatively inexpensive recorders, using small tape reels or cassettes, can produce good results but their slow recording speed makes it difficult to record high-frequency calls. The cassette tape cannot be edited, so the recording must be copied on to a master tape on a standard machine if it is to be kept and edited into a series of recordings.

Air rushing over the snipe's extended tail feathers makes a bleating sound.

MICROPHONES

To obtain as high-quality a reproduction as possible, not only must the recorder be as expensive as you can afford, but also the microphone must be chosen with care. Usually the microphone supplied is of the cheaper crystal type which picks up sound from all directions. The ribbon microphone picks up sound from in front and behind, but is useless in the field because it is very sensitive to wind (a breeze can sound like a gale). A moving coil microphone is best; directional and omni-directional types are available.

Be sure, by checking with your dealer, that your microphone is the type that can be used with an extension cable. This will probably be essential. Although good results can be achieved without it, much more can be attempted with it. The microphone can be placed at a chosen spot and the recordist can retire to a hideaway at a safe distance. The spot will have been selected after careful observation of the bird in question, noting song posts and possible microphone sites. However, good results can be achieved by other means. It can be exciting and rewarding to stalk your quarry, microphone in hand. Or you can hide in a suitable corner of a wood or seashore, hang your microphone somewhere handy, and wait for the birds to come to you. This can be especially good if you know you are by a regularly used drinking pool or wader roost.

A parabolic reflector enables sound to be collected from some distance.

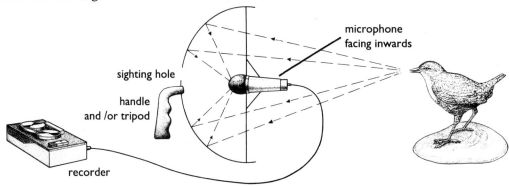

sighting hole

handle and /or tripod

microphone facing inwards

recorder

PROJECT 14

Recording bird song in the field using a parabolic reflector.

REFLECTORS

This is one last piece of equipment you may like to buy or perhaps even make for yourself. Although fine results can be obtained by using an open microphone (some professional and keen amateur recordists always work this way), many agree that a parabolic reflector is a great asset. It enables you to collect sound from some distance over its bowl shape, thus giving a strengthened signal to the microphone. A second benefit is that you can aim the reflector at a particular sound. The greater the reflector's diameter, the greater its range, but 46– 61 cm (18–24 in) is most manageable. Quite a good one can be made from an old bowl electric fire, or the back of a large old-fashioned car headlamp.

Low sounds, such as from a bittern or grasshopper warbler, cannot be magnified using the parabolic reflector, and an open microphone must be used.

FURTHER TIPS

Each recording should have a note of the date, time, place and weather, so that adequate comparisons can be made, if necessary, with other recordings.

Some final hints: patience and preparation are needed. Try to avoid recording on a windy day. Make sure you set the machine's recording level correctly. Above all, avoid disturbing the wildlife you hope to record. You may be disappointed at first because you find that too many strange noises have been recorded – a car, dogs barking, children shouting. The remedy is either to go somewhere quieter or to get up before anyone else does! Birds are early risers (*see* Project 16).

Having made a satisfactory recording – satisfactory according to your own standards, and later more 'professional' standards – the recordist's first aim may be to collect a call and song from as many species as possible. This is personally satisfying, and is far more conservation-minded than schoolboy egg-collecting, or stuffed-bird collecting which is sadly still all the rage in several Mediterranean countries.

Once the birdwatcher has gained confidence and a measure of expertise, the sound recordings collected could be used to further particular studies, such as those in Projects 15 to 18, which can be tackled well only by an observer who can confidently identify most of what he or she hears.

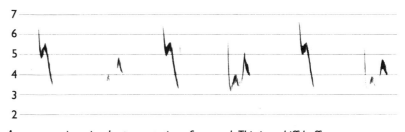

A sonogram is a visual representation of a sound. This is a chiffchaff song.

Hard to Tell Apart

Just when the birdwatcher is thinking that identifying bird songs is not so difficult, he will discover the problems in sorting out *Acrocephalus* warblers.

Closely related birds often have calls and songs that seem, to human ears, to be identical, but which on very careful listening may reveal subtle differences of tone, pitch or timing. This project is further preparation for any of the scientific projects which follow and which expect a high standard of identification of calls and songs. The list below is not in order of difficulty (it features common birds), but the measure of difficulty of sorting out each group will depend on the acuteness of one's hearing and application to the task.

comparative investigations into such questions as 'What is the difference between the tits' two-note songs?' and 'Which pipit's song is simplest and which is the most developed?'

SORT OUT THE SONGS OF:

1. Blackbird, song thrush, mistle thrush.
2. Tree pipit, meadow pipit, rock pipit.
3. Sedge and reed warblers.
4. Blackcap and garden warbler.
5. Marsh tit, great tit, coal tit.

AND THE CALLS OF:

6. Chiffchaff, willow warbler, wood warbler.
7. Waders in winter quarters.
8. The five common species of gulls.
9. Jackdaw, rook and carrion crow.
10. Moorhen and coot.

These learning projects could simply be used to familiarize the observer with the songs and calls, or else one or more could eventually develop into analytical and

*The three 'leaf' warblers, willow warbler (**top**), wood warbler (**middle**) and chiffchaff (**bottom**), are notoriously difficult to identify until they call or sing.*

Singing Marathon

To study bird-song properly, an ornithologist must be prepared to do field work all day, all night, all year round.

The passerines (that is the order of birds popularly called 'perching birds' or 'songbirds') are prodigious singers. Some idea of this can be understood if the bird-watcher makes notes throughout the year of each species singing every day in a given area. After twelve months, an analysis of the records can be drawn up by hand or with the help of a computer graphics programme. This can be checked with published records to see whether your bird is typical or not.

Closely related species can be compared. One statistical analysis of bird song has shown that the wren was the only study species to sing in every month. Do you agree?

A small bird such as a warbler, weighing about 12g (0.5oz), may sing in May or June from dawn until dusk, singing basically the same song perhaps 2,000 times.

Brown and Wolfendale (1948) watched and listened during a complete twenty-four hours in late April. This marathon gave the amazing results that the sedge warbler sang in every hour of the twenty-four, and in nine of those hours it sang in every minute. It sang more at night than did a nightingale! However, the same scientists discovered that the nightingale did sing mostly at night. These authors studied only the chaffinch, whitethroat, garden warbler, sedge warbler and nightingale. That gives plenty of scope for further research.

If that time-scale is too daunting, try an hour or so on one species. A blackcap that I studied one June sang, on average, 4.2 songs per minute. That was in mid-afternoon. Was it typical? How does it compare with song in April or May? Or early in the morning? Or in northern Britain?

(mine was in Devon, in south-west England).

The dawn chorus is a thrilling sound, albeit at three or four o'clock in the morning! On average the blackbird sings first, three quarters of an hour before sunrise, but one May I heard a song thrush that regularly started first at about 3.15 a.m. Study of your local dawn chorus would repay the early rise.

Dawn (and therefore dusk) makes one think of a rather difficult, technical study: the investigation of a bird's song in relation to the day length. The chosen bird's song output would need to be noted carefully throughout the day and compared with equally carefully taken measurements made with a good photographic light meter. An idea would be gained then of the relationship, if any, between song output and light intensity. Alternatively the variable could be rainfall or temperature – or all three.

Finally, this project's title 'Marathon' implies distance as well as duration. At what range are various songbirds easily audible? Wrens can be heard at a distance of half a mile in good conditions. Does that make them the loudest of European songbirds? Very little is known of this aspect of bird song.

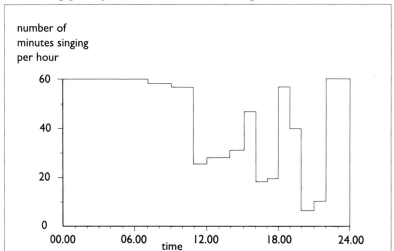

Sedge warbler song chart for a complete twenty-four hours. It is clear that most of its singing is performed at night and in the early morning.

Dialects and Mimicry

Birds' songs are not fixed, unchangeable sounds. One song thrush's song is not exactly like another's, even though both are recognizably song thrush.

It is well known that birds have dialects. A collection and comparison of the dialects of a species would be interesting. The chaffinch and song thrush are good subjects; so is the wren. It has been noted that British island populations of the wren have distinctive songs especially on the Hebrides and St Kilda.

To be sure that one bird has a local dialect, many recordings from several areas will need to be made and song patterns learned (for example one individual chaffinch may have five different songs, all recognizably chaffinch because of the typical shape of the phrases plus the terminal flourish). Only careful study will reveal a local dialect, rather than a song type, which is simply part of the bird's repertoire.

Perhaps one of the most intriguing vocabularies is that of the starling, whose endless gurgles, warbles, wheezes and splutters would make a fascinating recording if coupled with a careful analysis explaining the circumstances of each sound.

Several species are known to mimic other birds or even non-avian sounds. Especially well-known examples are the superb lyrebird of Australia, the mockingbird of North America, and the European starling. There is evidence to suggest that mockingbirds and lyrebirds pick up the sounds in the neighbourhood. A starling that I heard by my suburban house was whistling the curlew's call, *cour-lee*, which it could not have heard locally but must have learned elsewhere, in winter probably.

The problem is to identify the calls that are not natural to the songster. The marsh warbler has been studied and shown to copy not only European birds where it breeds, but African birds where it winters! Its relatives, the sedge and reed warblers are good mimics and would be worth detailed study, and so possibly would the jay, wheatear and redstart.

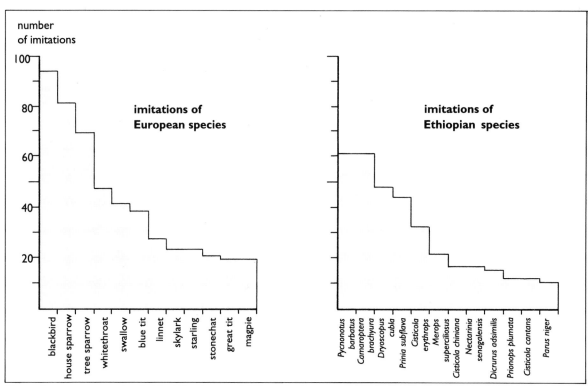

The twelve most commonly mimicked European and African species recorded from one marsh warbler in just forty minutes of continuous song (Lemaire, 1979).

Duets and Subsong

It is often assumed that only cock birds sing, and that suddenly, when adult, they can do it. But some hens sing; and individuals have to learn what to sing.

The editors of *The Birds of the Western Palaearctic* have admitted that an investigation of female song and the possibilities of more duetting in species in Europe would be good topics for study amongst others to improve our understanding of the rôles of the sexes. Female bird singers worth studying would be bullfinch, swallow, robin and crossbill (if by colour-ringing you can be sure of identifying a hen later on, *see* Project 51).

In duets, or antiphonal calling, the vocalizations of the male and female follow each other so quickly that unless you knew better you would not believe two birds were involved. The most famous examples are found in the tropics. In England I have heard a duet of alarm calls from a pair of wood warblers, anxious at the arrival of a jay near their nest. First I heard the plaintive *piu, piu*, two notes oft-repeated. Then I realized the first note was higher-pitched than the second.

Eventually I tracked down *two* birds and discovered that each was calling one note, right after the other in perfect, repeated rhythm. What other British birds duet?

CHARACTERISTICS OF SUBSONG WHICH MAKE IT DIFFERENT FROM FULL SONG

1. It is quiet or very quiet.
2. It is of a different pattern.
3. The song bursts are longer.
4. The notes are of a lower frequency.
5. The notes are less pure in tone and less definite in pitch.
6. It is usually produced when sexual motivation is low.
7. In young birds at least it appears to be a form of practice.

Sometimes one is aware of very quiet songs that differ radically from the loud, full territorial songs, and they can be identified only when the bird is seen. This is subsong. Quiet, inward songs that are similar to the full song should be called whispering songs. Needless to say such groups are very hard to hear because they are audible at only a metre or two. I have heard subsong regularly only from the robin and blackbird (several of my records note the male was a black-beaked immature, the beak was closed, and the only sign to show that the faint warbling belonged to the bird being watched was my seeing its throat quivering).

I have also heard subsong from blackcap, song thrush, dunnock, chiffchaff, willow warbler and chaffinch; and whispering song from the blackbird and willow warbler.

It has been remarked that the robin's subdued song in autumn was a puzzling feature of the song of the species. My experience of a juvenile, speckled-plumage robin and an immature blackbird subsinging adds weight to characteristic (7) in the panel, and perhaps solves the puzzle. Further research by anyone with good hearing would be well worthwhile, even for the blackbird and chaffinch for which perhaps most evidence is available.

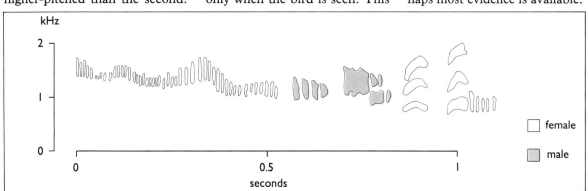

The diagram shows a performance by a pair of slate-coloured boubou shrikes from Africa. When the birds call one after the other it is known as antiphonal singing; sometimes they do duet singing together (Seibt and Wickler, 1977).

4. FOOD AND FEEDING HABITS

Many people regularly feed birds at bird-tables in full view of their living rooms, and so they have ready-made laboratories in which to pursue detailed scientific investigations.

Garden birds are often fed in a haphazard manner, and in ignorance of the birds' requirements. Much has been done by Tony Soper to redress the situation and it is assumed that his book, *The Bird Table Book*, and the BTO's *Garden Bird Book* have been studied before the projects in this chapter are tackled.

Most bird books mention what birds eat, but the information is often presented vaguely as 'insects and

spiders' or 'small seeds and occasionally berries'. The new *Birds of the Western Palaearctic* has detailed notes for most species (*see* example below); some notes include anecdotal information such as 'one record of lizard *Lacerta agilis*' (for wheatear) and 'recorded following a tractor ploughing field covered with tall weeds and taking insects disturbed' (for swallow). That such records are published in such a distinguished work shows that every birdwatcher can expect sooner or later to record a novelty of feeding behaviour. Publish it in *British Birds* or *Bird Watching* or the local ornithological society's report, and later help someone's detailed research into the life of a particular

Some ducks, such as this female mallard, do not dive but 'up-end' to reach food.

HOW MUCH DOES A DUNNOCK EAT?

May–October	November–April
Beetles 62%	Beetles 73%
Spiders 29%	Spiders 12%
Earthworms 4%	Snails 7%
Diptera (flies) 3%	Springtails 4.5%
Snails 2%	Earthworms 3.5%
Springtails 1%	

Figures refer to approximate percentages of invertebrates in faecal remains.

From May to July no seeds present in faeces, but otherwise between 60 per cent and 90 per cent of the food is seeds. Percentages can be deceiving! (Data from Cramp, 1988.)

This redshank is feeding by treading mud which stirs up food.

species. Many short notes in magazines are not precise enough to help an enthusiastic student because they are generally unusual records of food or feeding behaviour. Many books do give qualitative information, naming prey species, but rarely give quantitative information about how much of each type of food is eaten. The late James Fisher in his encyclopedic book *The Fulmar* quoted only one quantitative food record compared with over twenty pages describing what prey species had been eaten, and that is still largely the sum of our knowledge for this large petrel. In September 1971, I watched a blue tit eating ripe elderberries, which was then a novel observation for me. Hollom says that the species eats 'fruit'; Coward does not mention fruit but does give more detail of other foods; Bannerman admits that blue tits eat 'some fruit' but names none; Perrins does record that they ate elderberries in September in an Oxfordshire wood, with 30 per cent or more of the birds recorded being seen in elders in September (see Project 23), which all leaves me still wondering – how important to blue tits are elderberries?

It must be admitted that behavioural studies, censusing and nest-watching can be much easier work than food investigations. Bird food is often small, hard to identify (for example small insects and their larvae), and difficult to study over any length of time or in particular habitats. This is especially true of species that wander from place to place (try following a feeding flock of linnets, or waders on a mudflat, or swallows in the air!). But although the professional birdwatcher, who can spend all day and every day at this sort of study and has extra knowledge and facilities, seems to have an advantage, amateurs throughout the years since serious ornithology began have made studies of the greatest detail and value which would have done credit to any professional scientist.

Gibb and Hartley, in a valuable review of bird foods and feeding habits, pointed out that 'the proportions of different foods in the diet of most species of birds are still all to learn', and in this quantitative study of birds' foods and feeding habits, the amateur ornithologist can make important contributions to the study of bird ecology and behaviour. The immediate aim may be either to tell 'the plain tale' of a relation between predator and prey as part of the biology of a single species, or to study a problem of ecology comparing the feeding habits of one species with those of another.

Compared with the dozens of bird books now in print about identification, behaviour and distribution, only two come to mind which are about food: *Birds and Berries* (1989), by B and D Snow, and *Gulls and Plovers* (1985), by C Barnard and D Thompson, which is about the ecology and behaviour of mixed-species feeding groups. Perhaps your studies will be the basis of the next title.

Bird-Tables and Feeding Stations

Undoubtedly the surest way to watch birds closely in your garden is to attract them regularly to a well-stocked bird-table.

DESIGNING AND SITING A TABLE

Although a bird-table can be made cheaply, it will pay you either to buy a good one (from the catalogue of the Royal Society for the Protection of Birds, for example) or, if you want to make your own, to use timber that will withstand all the changes of weather it will have to endure in a year. Ask your local timber merchant's advice, and find out what off-cuts he has.

A simple design is best: a tray about 50cm x 30cm (20in x 12in) on the top of a pole. You should avoid the so-called 'rustic' tables often advertised or seen at garden centres. The thatched rooves will soon spoil; the free-standing versions are not very stable; those with a built-in nestbox in the roof are especially unsuitable (a blue tit taking over the box in the New Year, as they often do, would have a dreadful time defending it against all comers to the table below).

Be careful where you site the table. Many garden birdwatchers like their bird-tables as near as possible to their windows so that the visiting birds can be observed closely. Indeed, many a successful table has been fixed to a window-sill, even to an upper-floor sill of a flat. Ideally the table needs to be sited so that the birds can reach it by way of a series of short flights from bush to bush. For safety's sake, do not place it in the middle of the lawn - in full view of a predator such as a sparrowhawk, or near a wall from which a cat can pounce.

FOODSTUFFS

If you want to attract a variety of birds you must provide a variety of food. Many people object to the starlings, jackdaws, sparrows or even gulls which gobble all the bird food (kitchen scraps and bread). Different species need different diets. A pet shop's wild-bird food will be a good start. It should contain seeds and grains that the starlings will not touch, but the dunnocks and finches will love. Blue tits and great tits will come all winter to peanuts hung in a special feeder, and if you live in suburbia or in a rural area, you will probably get siskins, greenfinches and nuthatches on them too. Coal tits love sunflower seeds. If your garden is large enough, you can arrange one bird-table for scraps and fat, another for seed; hanging containers of peanuts; and seed on the ground for birds like the dunnock, chaffinch and collared dove, which are normally ground feeders. Good, experienced suppliers of wild-bird food will also sell, at a price, specially blended mixtures for insectivorous birds such as robins and wrens; and 'songster food' for other non seed-eaters such as blackbirds and song thrushes. In the autumn and winter, the

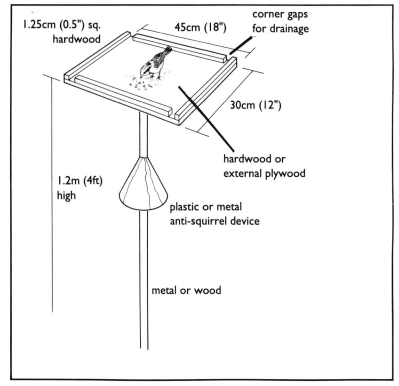

1.25cm (0.5") sq. hardwood

45cm (18")

corner gaps for drainage

30cm (12")

hardwood or external plywood

1.2m (4ft) high

plastic or metal anti-squirrel device

metal or wood

A simply-designed bird-table. Note the gaps in the surround at the corners to allow water to drain away.

thrushes love to feed on windfall apples.

Once you start to get regular visitors to your table, they must be fed regularly. They may come to rely on your food source and may depend on it in poor weather. It is as well, however, *not* to put out bulky foods from May to August: tits feed their young on small caterpillars, and peanuts and bread are indigestible to the young and will kill them. If the autumn gives a good crop of berries and seeds, the birds may stay in the hedges and fields and your peanuts will go mouldy in the holder and the uneaten seed on the table will sprout after rain! When the weather deteriorates and food is scarce the birds will soon return.

BUYING BIRD FOOD

Ideally you should buy your food from a supplier who displays the Birdfood Standards Associations Seal of Approval or Seal of Superior Quality, both of which are supported by the RSPB and the BTO. Such suppliers regularly advertise in the publications of these two organizations.

HYGIENE

You should clear the bird-table and food receptacles regularly, and rotate ground feeding areas.

WATER SOURCE

A source of water is as important in a bird garden as the food. Birds need to drink – some more than others – and to bathe, to freshen their plumage (*see* Project 36). If you have a garden pond, it will need a shallow end about 5cm (6in) deep or less with sloping sides; otherwise a bird-bath is ideal. Always keep the water fresh. In winter, *never* add an anti-freeze agent: it will kill the birds. Just keep putting out fresh water!

Some birdwatchers, particularly those in more rural areas, may be lucky enough to attract marsh tits to their bird-table along with the commoner blue, great and coal tits.

43

Garden Bird Survey I

Careful recording of the birds at a feeding station can reveal interesting statistics to do with the relative abundance of species and regularity of visits.

Once the feeding station, that is the bird-table, hanging container or the regular seed supply on the ground, is established it is satisfying to keep a list of all species that come to it. It is particularly exciting when a rarity occurs such as the black redstart I had once, and the reed buntings which come with the chaffinches during a cold spell. Other birdwatchers have recorded woodcock, water rail and merlin, and herons regularly visit well-stocked goldfish ponds even in suburbia miles from a river!

However, it is interesting to learn more about the feeding birds, rather than merely listing them. Careful noting throughout the year at regular times will give a statistical account of the relative abundance of each species. The method of counting is worth considering carefully: a different method might give a wildly different result. For example, noting each species present per week might show the result expressed as example 1 in the table below.

Clearly the sparrow and blue tit were most frequently seen.

HOW MANY SPECIES OF BIRDS VISIT GARDENS?

The following data show the average number of species seen per garden in a national survey.

Winter 1988/89

	Rural	Suburban
	20.2	18.2
(range)	10–30	9–30

Summer 1988/89

	Rural	Suburban
	20.5	15.5
(range)	7–34	2–30

(Data from the BTO's national Garden Bird Survey.)

The blue tit is one of the most common birds recorded at feeders.

EXAMPLES OF TWO WAYS OF MEASURING THE RELATIVE ABUNDANCE OF SPECIES IN THE GARDEN

Example 1: simple presence only measurement

Week	Species seen			
1st	house sparrow	starling	blue tit	—
2nd	"	"	—	—
3rd	"	—	"	wren
4th	"	—	"	dunnock
5th	"	—	"	chaffinch
Total units	5	2	4	1, 1, 1

Example 2: maximum peak count of each species seen per week

Week	Species seen			
1st	5 house sparrows	9 starlings	1 blue tit	—
2nd	2 "	14 "	—	—
3rd	4 "	—	1 "	1 wren
4th	3 "	—	2 "	1 dunnock
5th	6 "	—	2 "	2 chaffinches
Total	20	23	6	1, 1, 2

But were they the most abundant? More detailed watching and a different recording technique might give the result shown as example 2 in the table at the bottom of the previous page.

Although the same birds are involved, the relative abundance of the species is shown differently. Tits seem to be much less abundant than sparrows although they were nearly as regularly seen. Statistical work at the feeding station depends on the observer's curiosity, patience and endurance, and just how determined he is to discover more about his population of garden birds.

Cowie and Hinsley (1988) surveyed nearly 300 gardens in Cardiff to discover the extent to which householders provided food for birds. They suggest that 'those interested in the welfare of garden birds should provide more food in August and September … when the demand by fledged young remains high'. They would like to hear from anyone thinking about doing a similar survey.

It is important to enable birds, like this blackbird, to bathe.

A GARDEN BIRD FEEDING QUESTIONNAIRE

with acknowledgement to Richard Cowie, Department of Zoology, University College, PO Box 78, Cardiff CF11 1XL.

FROM...(your name) OF..
....
(your address)
Questionnaire: garden bird feeding survey. Please fill in the information required or ring the appropriate answer.

FEEDING BIRDS

1. Please circle the month when you feed the birds:
   Jan Feb Mar Apr May Jun Jul Aug Sep Oct Nov Dec

2. How often do you feed the birds in winter and summer? Place a tick in the appropriate place:

	Oct–Mar	Apr–Sep
a) at least once a day	....	....
b) several times a week	....	....
c) occasionally	....	....
d) not at all	....	....

3. Please indicate which foods you put out in winter and summer:

	Oct–Mar	Apr–Sep
a) peanuts	....	....
b) bread	....	....
c) fat	....	....
d) household scraps	....	....
e) proprietary bird food	....	....
f) other (please specify)	....	....

4. Do you put food out:
   a) on the ground ....
   b) on the bird-table ....
   c) in a peanut holder ....
   d) other (please specify) ....

5. Other information
   a) do you provide water for the birds? Yes/No
   b) how many dogs do you own? ....
   c) how many cats do you own? ....
   d) how many *other* cats visit your garden? ....
   e) if you own a cat/cats how many birds did it/they catch last year? ....
   f) any other comment?

I will collect the questionnaire in a week's time

Garden Bird Survey II

Co-ordinated surveys of garden birds, organized by bird clubs can provide a wealth of information, which can help in the conservation of our garden visitors.

In the winter of 1967–68 members of the Devon and Cornwall birdwatching societies carried out a survey of birds visiting bird-tables and ground stations. The results gave for the first time quantitative information about the garden birds of south-west England.

TOP TWELVE GARDEN BIRDS IN SW ENGLAND 1967–68	
Robin	99%
Blue tit	99%
Blackbird	98%
Great tit	96%
Starling	96%
House sparrow	94%
Dunnock	90%
Greenfinch	79%
Song thrush	78%
Coal tit	77%
Chaffinch	69%
Marsh tit	38%
% = percentage of tables visited from the total of 127.	

Twenty years later, the BTO's Garden Bird Survey was in its final year of three (*see* panel above right)

The top species have maintained their positions. But in 1968 the magpie was seen at only 16 per cent of feeding stations, and the collared dove at 18 per cent. And now where are the marsh tits and song thrushes? A European garden bird survey in the winter of 1987–88 found that the great tit was the most ubiquitous bird and the house sparrow was most abundant.

TOP TWELVE RURAL GARDEN BIRDS IN SW ENGLAND IN AUTUMN 1989	
Blue tit	91%
Robin	90%
Blackbird	88%
Great tit	82%
House sparrow	78%
Chaffinch	75%
Starling	69%
Wren	68%
Dunnock	66%
Magpie	54%
Greenfinch	53%
Collared dove	50%
% = average percentage of gardens visited.	

If you make careful notes, your survey can illustrate how the use birds make of your bird-table may be influenced by weather conditions. This will mean you noting maximum and minimum temperatures (with a good outdoor thermometer from your local garden centre), wind direction and strength, and rainfall and sunshine amounts. Many birdwatchers save each day the weather maps from a quality newspaper (this is very important to help you interpret cold weather movements and migration – *see* also Project 38). If the survey is wide enough, geographical variations can be analysed. In your own garden, valuable information can be collected by comparing the frequency with which certain species do take food; by studying the species that come regularly to the garden but usually take only natural food (for example, wren and long-tailed tit); by comparing the 'character' of different species and discovering which are social and will tolerate others at the table, including their own species, and which are loners and come only when the table is clear (*see* Project 24).

In the autumn of 1991, the BTO launched its new Garden Bird Enquiry. It is proposed to

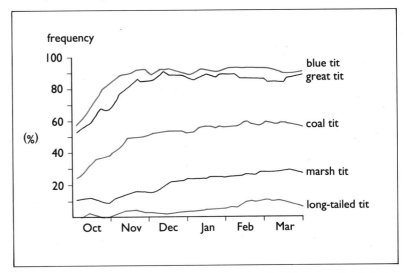

The relative abundance of five species of tits at bird-tables. The vertical scale is the percentage of tables visited by each species (Penwarden, 1969).

PROJECT 21

EUROPEAN GARDEN BIRD SURVEY, OCTOBER 1988 TO MAY 1989

Area	No. of gardens surveyed	No. of species seen at least once	Most frequently seen species	Most abundant species	Special notes
Fenno-Scandinavia	118	106	great tit	greenfinch	seed-eaters seen here more than any other region
West Germany & Austria	121	91	great tit	house sparrow	woodpigeon seen more than in any other region
Spain, Italy & Portugal	60	118	robin	house sparrow	chiffchaff, blackcap and black redstart seen regularly
France & Switzerland	61	103	great tit	house sparrow	nuthatch and marsh tit were frequent visitors
Netherlands & Belgium	54	82	great tit	house sparrow	only in this region was the starling in the top twelve
Eire	26	53	blue tit	greenfinch	many species found in UK are absent in Eire

(Data from *BTO News* no. 166, January 1990.)

make this a long-term project, based on a survey of between 600 and 800 gardens, selected according to their size, garden type and where they are in Britain. It is intended to maintain the collection of information from the greatest variety of types of gardens with the greatest geographical spread. The survey cards are easy to fill in, computer readable and will allow the BTO to collect more information about garden birds than ever before, analyse it quickly and publish the results in a newsletter and scientific papers. If you would like observations in your garden to be considered, write to the BTO (*see* page 125 for their address).

The basic requirement in a garden birds survey is that birds should be coming to food deliberately put out for them within a defined area that can be watched regularly. The observer should record the highest number (peak count) of birds of each species seen feeding or drinking each week. One way to do this is to hang a notepad or washable pad in a convenient place, list likely species down the left-hand side, and days across the top, starting at Sunday. By splitting Saturday and Sunday you lessen the weekend bias in the amount of watching and counting you are likely to do. Record each day's highest count, then at the end of the week select the highest number and enter that on the master sheet. Analysis of the results can be shown in graphs, histograms or pie-charts.

Wild-bird seed from suppliers varies greatly in the proportion of each grain and seed in the mixture. You could experiment to find out from the range of seeds on offer which the birds prefer, and so overcome the expense of having the grain, millet or sunflower seeds wasted.

The great tit is perhaps the most frequently seen and attractive garden bird throughout much of northern and central Europe. This one is taking food to young in a natural nest hole.

How Many Meals?

We traditionally think of ourselves as having three main meals a day. But how many meals does a bird need?

How long is a bird's meal? How often does it feed? Studies at Wytham Wood, Oxfordshire, by scientists at Oxford University, have shown that an adult great tit may make over 600 visits to a nestbox to feed the young; a pair of buzzards on Dartmoor brought food to their young at rates varying from three kills in twenty-three minutes one day, to none in twenty-four hours.

It is not too difficult to find out by watching from a hide how often chicks at a nest are fed. Those with a flair for mechanics can construct a counting mechanism to do the hard work for them with hole-nesting birds. It is even possible to make a counter at an open nest in a bush or tree by placing twigs over 'in' and 'out' perches connected to a counter. This idea has worked well at a mistle thrush's nest.

Gulls, ducks and waders on mudflats, or birds in a wood, are more difficult to study than birds at a nest. It is often not easy to see when the bird has found food. Black-headed gulls are widespread in autumn and winter and are often quite approachable. One August, I watched one, through binoculars, for nearly twenty minutes. It walked at a steady pace on an erratic course across the mudflat, picking at the surface methodically, and getting a food-item at almost every peck, with very few misses. Successful pecks were clear because a little worm could be seen at the tip of the bill. The gull foot-paddled in a pool it came on by chance as it meandered across the mud. No food was washed before it was swallowed (compare that with some waders: they regularly wash food before swallowing it).

> ### A BLACK-HEADED GULL'S MID-AFTERNOON MEAL
>
> One hundred worms in eight minutes. Paused at number sixty-seven in a pool, but pushed on by another gull. Then 100 worms in 4.5 minutes and sixty-seven worms in six minutes, after which it flew off of its own accord.
>
> (River Severn, 24th August 1986. See also Project 28.)

It is often not easy to see when a bird has found food and all the observer's ingenuity will be necessary to obtain the information he needs. Starlings are easy to watch feeding in flocks in open grassy areas: on 30 August 1970 I watched ten on my front lawn probe for and dig up twenty-seven leatherjackets in seven minutes before they flew off. Unfortunately, I did not record the number of unsuccessful probes. It would be interesting to find time to watch other groups and compare their feeding success. Canada geese and mute swans are widespread and easy to watch. How much time do they spend feeding compared to preening and resting?

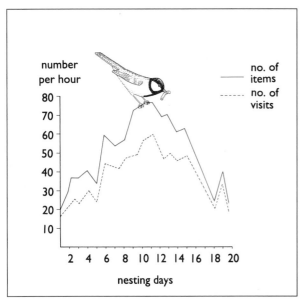

Rate of feeding of a brood of great tits. The observations were made at an observation nestbox with a glass back, the box being attached to a hide. A full description of such a hide is given in Project 6 (Betts, 1955).

Starlings feeding on short turf among a flock of sheep.

Feeding Together

Although there are some particularly well-known overseas birds which depend on other animals to help them get food, little is known about British birds that behave like this.

When creatures of different species live together and render mutual assistance this is known as symbiosis, from the Greek meaning 'a living together'. Several examples are well known. A greater honeyguide will lead a ratel (a badger-like animal) to a bees' nest, then eat the wax combs after the ratel has had the honey. Oxpeckers in Africa hunt for ticks from the backs of many species of animals, acting as lookouts in return.

When two species live together but only one seems to get any benefit, this is known as commensalism. Perhaps the best avian example of this is the carmine bee-eater's use of the kori bustard as a travelling perch in the African savanna. The bustard disturbs insects and the bee-eater dives off its host to snap up the meal. This is picturesquely called hitch-hiking.

It is perhaps not so well known that similar relationships

SYMBIOTIC RELATIONSHIP BETWEEN A DABCHICK AND TUFTED DUCK

From 12.20 to 12.30, a dabchick was very closely associated with a female tufted duck. The dabchick kept within about 15cm (6 in) of the duck. When the duck dived, the dabchick dived. When both rose, the dabchick always paddled to be close by the duck, facing the same way.

They dived twelve times in ten minutes, plus two extra dives by the dabchick when the duck did not rise. The dabchick always dived second, and rose first. The partnership broke up when the duck paddled to what seemed to be deeper water and preened.

The dabchick worked with a drake for two dives, then saw the same duck and paddled about 100m (110 yds) to be close by for two dives. A second dabchick paddled in and trilled at the first who swam away. Dabchick '2' dived once with the duck; '1' trilled and closed in. Both then left the duck and swam to the cover of some nearby overhanging trees.

The dabchick was presumably benefiting from the bigger bird's dive which disturbed more food than the duck could catch and eat by itself.

---

exist in North America and Britain. Yellow wagtails and starlings will feed under the noses of cattle, eating insects disturbed by the cows. I have seen a yellow wagtail fly-catching so close to a cow's nose that the beast sneezed, presumably with irritation, and blew the wagtail out of the way! Hawfinches have been observed following thrushes or golden orioles, feeding on the seeds or stones that these birds discard from the fruit they eat. Greenfinches have been observed eating the flesh of *Rosa rugosa* fruits and marsh tits the seeds.

It may be that other symbiotic and commensal feeding relationships will come to light if we watch carefully. With regard to those already discovered, it would be interesting to know exactly what happens. Very careful observation might reveal how much more advantageous it is, for example, for starlings and yellow wagtails to follow cattle, than to feed in areas where there are none; and whether the habit is regular or occasional. A good subject for study would be starlings and members of the crow family, especially jackdaws and magpies, feeding on the backs of sheep, cattle and even deer. Birdwatchers lucky enough to travel to southern Europe or Africa can watch cattle egrets doing the same thing.

Careful observation revealed that treecreepers that associate with tit flocks are able to be less vigilant and so spend more time feeding. Who else helps whom in a wood? Do symbiotic relationships occur on the seashore or tideline among birds turning over pebbles or seaweed?

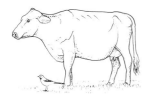

Pied and yellow wagtails often feed near cattle on the insects they disturb.

Peck Order

A flock or smaller group of birds may look like a formless collection of individuals, but a set of rules is in fact keeping them in safe order.

Starlings on the lawn are, to the untrained observer, always squabbling. They do indeed jostle each other and voice a constant bickering chatter when the flock descends on the table. A fieldfare in my garden one winter ate almost nothing and spent most of twenty minutes chasing others away from its rosehips, so that it could feed on them itself later. Birds that feed in flocks – gulls, waders, starlings, thrushes and rooks – normally keep apart from each other, just far enough to avoid squabbling (*see* project 22). This space between birds is called 'the individual distance'. For black-headed gulls, it is about 30cm (12in). By careful observation, try to find the individual distance for a variety of species: skylarks on stubble, linnets on weeds, winter thrushes, goldfinches on thistles, starlings on a lawn or field, rooks in a pasture, waders on a mudflat, tufted ducks on a lake, or pigeons on fallen grain.

TWO BIRD-TABLE PECK ORDERS			
1	jackdaw	1	great and blue tits
2	nuthatch	2	marsh tit
3	blue tit	3	nuthatch
4	great tit	4	starling
5	robin	5	coal tit
6	dunnock	6	house sparrow
7	chaffinch	7	blackbird & robin
8	coal tit (shy)	8	dunnock & chaffinch
9	blackbird	9	magpie

Besides the flock keeping itself in order through observing the individual distance rule, birds do also dominate each other by aggressive behaviour, which is recognized not only by their congeners but also by other species. Anyone who keeps or has kept hens knows that certain birds dominate others. There is a set hierarchy or rank order among the birds which they work out for themselves by aggressive display. This is usually called the 'peck order'. Peck orders are not well studied in the wild but two quoted by Mr and Mrs Penwar-

den (1969; *see* table) show which species dominate others.

A careful detailed study of peck orders could probably be done only after a comprehensive programme of colour-ringing to identify individual birds (*see* Projects 50 and 51). This would help to show whether a species was always dominant (or subordinate) or just whether certain individuals of any species had strong or weak characters. Watching thrushes in winter feeding on fallen fruit in an orchard will reveal peck orders. One of the most interesting accounts of peck orders is that described by Lorenz for jackdaws in his book *King Solomon's Ring* published in 1952.

How aggressive is the sedge warbler towards other species?

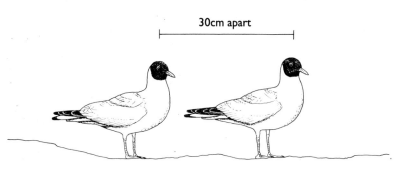

30cm apart

Black-headed gulls lined up on a roof, railings or jetty show the principle of individual distance very well. They will usually all be facing into the wind.

Flowerpeckers

Some species have very specialized feeding habits which are generally known but have not been studied in detail even in well-watched Western Europe.

It is often reported that house sparrows nibble at flowers in spring, especially primroses and primulas. Recently a correspondent to a radio programme mentioned seeing a blue tit and a robin picking flowers, but could find no trace of them in the nearby nests to which they had been taken. Did they and the sparrows eat the flowers? Were they searching for seed, insects or nectar? My own notes are inconclusive. My primroses' stems have been pecked through and the blooms left lying in some years but not others. I have seen only house sparrows doing it. It is likely that an investigation of flowerpecking will not be found to be a food study but a behavioural one. In the last few years starlings on the Isles of Scilly have learned to sup nectar in late summer from the brilliant red flowers of the New Zealand pohutukawa tree. Birds are often found adapting to new situations. Are some sparrows finding a new food source obtainable by a method similar to that used by flower-piercers and bananaquits of Central and South America? From what other nectar-producing flowers are sparrows learning to feed?

Kay (1985) believes that 'bird–plant attractions are not so well known as they ought to be. Nectar is a potential food source to birds, while the plants could also benefit from having the birds act as pollinators'. Kay's investigations showed that a blue tit needed to feed on catkin nectar for between three and four hours only to get all its energy requirements for the day. Every spring, tits visit my garden's willows. How often do you see tits among the catkins? What species are they? Are they nectar-feeding or insect-gathering? Dr Kay believes the blue tit is the only European example of significant bird-pollination of a native plant in Europe.

NECTAR FEEDERS? POLLINATORS?

These birds have been recorded with pollen on their heads:

Blackcap
Whitethroat
Chiffchaff
Willow warbler

The behaviour of these species towards flowers should be observed carefully. At present, we do not know for sure the answers to the questions in the text. Your observations could help solve the problem.

In North and tropical America, hummingbirds are fed from special feeders containing a sugary solution, as can be seen elsewhere in zoo aviaries. It would be interesting to put out such feeders in temperate climes in the hope of attracting starlings, or something unexpected, to a closely watched position. Perhaps then, it may be possible to discover whether this is a feeding habit that might catch on, in the same way as tits learned to open milk bottles on doorsteps. Experiments to find the optimum honey and water content of the feed would be of value in the wild, because although interesting in themselves, these experiments with hummingbirds were concerned only with aviary birds.

AN ARTIFICIAL FOOD MIXTURE FOR HUMMINGBIRDS, AND PERHAPS OTHER NECTAR FEEDERS

400%	Water
70%	honey
3%	protein
2%	fat
6%	trace elements, minerals, vitamins, roughage

% = percentage in relation to the bird's body weight.

APPROXIMATE WEIGHTS OF SOME POSSIBLE NECTAR FEEDERS

Great spotted woodpecker	85g (3oz)
Blue tit	12g (0.5oz)
Great tit	20g (0.75oz)
Blackcap	20g (0.75oz)
Willow warbler	10g (0.35oz)
Chiffchaff	9g (0.35oz)
Starling	90g (3.1oz)
Blackbird	100g (3.5oz)

Blue tits, blackbirds, nuthatches and great spotted woodpeckers have been attracted to honey solutions in holders sold by pet shops as drinking tubes for cage-birds, and blackbirds have been seen taking nectar from puja flowers on the Isles of Scilly, Cornwall.

Burying Food

Although it is well known that several species of birds bury food, very little is known about how much of this food is recovered.

Rooks and jays in particular are known to cache acorns when there is a surplus of this food. Cacheing has been recorded from September to December, but especially in October, when many acorns have fallen. Jays may be seen in autumn picking acorns off the tree and taking them to ground to bury in a near-by grassy area in a hole made by a stab of the bill. Sometimes carrion crows and magpies have been observed to cache bread thrown out in the garden.

It is also well-documented that coal tits and marsh tits regularly cache nuts and seeds, but blue tits and great tits rarely do. The storage habit is commonest where the birds have to endure cold winters, as in Scandinavia. It is clear that there is survival value in hiding food which is plentiful, in order to retrieve it when times are hard.

Careful watching with high-powered binoculars or a telescope will be needed to be sure that a food item has been either buried or retrieved. Very few studies have been made of the recovery of food. Is it really worth all the effort by the bird to bury it? Waite (1985) watched rooks searching for food on grassland. They found invertebrates, as expected, and acorns that were buried only occasionally, as if they found them by chance. In cold weather, acorns were found ten times more quickly.

KNOWN EXAMPLES OF FOOD STORAGE BY TITS	
Willow tits	dead-nettle seeds
Coal tits	small slugs, small caterpillars, and aphids (in little pellets of 20 to 25 aphids mixed with saliva), spruce seeds
Crested tits	as much as 20% of stored food as animal matter
Marsh tits	seeds

British tits will cache food on the ground in grass tussocks or moss, or behind bark. Where ground is regularly frozen or snow-covered (as in Scandinavia), bark crevices are most commonly used.

Very little is known still about the recovery of food buried by any species of bird. The easiest to study is probably the rook, which works in open fields where caches can be clearly seen and plotted. There is scope for an experiment with tits in a garden or wood, in putting out a set number of peanuts or sunflower seeds and counting carefully those which are taken (a) to be eaten and (b) to be stored. Good visibility is needed from the viewpoint to ensure that a tit can be watched from the feeding station to the landing point. Caches could be plotted on a large-scale map and follow-up visits made later to discover the recovery rate. If many birds make caches, random discovery by a roving flock will help all the seekers regardless of which bird hides which seed.

A jay digging in the snow and leaf-litter for acorns which it had buried in the previous autumn.

Stealing Food

We are all familiar with the story of the cuckoo stealing another bird's nest, but it is not so well known that many species steal another's meal.

Tits are inquisitive creatures, searching all sorts of nooks and crannies in order to find food. This has lead to their coming to the attention of the public when they even come indoors, tearing at wallpaper, presumably searching behind a peeled corner as they would peck away behind flakes of bark on a tree. Such activity was recorded even as long ago as the 17th century. Even more intriguing is the raiding of bottles of milk, which is practised today by several species. Householders are irritated by the despoiling of the day's milk, but birdwatchers are delighted!

What species steal milk in your district? Is the habit regular or seasonal? How widespread is the practice? Try compiling a questionnaire, delivering it to a selection of houses and collecting the papers a few days later. Ideally the houses chosen should either be all those in a given area, or a random selection chosen by a computer's random number selection programme.

Other forms of stealing are also worthy of note. As a part of Project 26 (*see* page 52) or as a separate effort, the garden or woodland birdwatcher could see how great a nuisance great tits are to other tits because they follow them and retrieve food that has just been cached.

One bird robbing another of food is frequently observed among birds, but is a regular habit only in a few. It is known as 'kleptoparasitism' or more commonly 'piracy'. Black-headed gulls will patrol a field with lapwings and golden plovers to steal the earthworms the plovers find; gulls will chase crows and jackdaws that have a tasty morsel; and I have watched a great black-backed gull circling, watching a gannet fishing, and diving in when the gannet surfaced to make it disgorge the fish.

The most famous pirates are skuas which feed by chasing gulls and terns, forcing them to disgorge their last meal which is then caught in flight. Gulls are

THE MILK-BOTTLE RAIDERS

Records of the habit exist across the land, from Rosshire to Gwynedd to Shropshire to Avon to Kent. Blue tits and great tits are commonly accused of pecking open the foil lids and sipping the cream but a recent BTO survey revealed that magpies, jackdaws, rooks and carrion crows were culprits too.

Magpies in Weston-super-Mare followed a milkman down the road. For at least five years, a Lancashire milkman has had to cover bottles. Elsewhere milk cartons, yoghurt, cream and egg-boxes have been raided. In Kent, an immature herring gull clumsily knocked over the bottles but magpies in Birmingham drank the cream as far as their beaks would reach without knocking bottles over!

(from BTO/BASF Garden Bird Survey, Newsletter April 1990)

closely related to skuas but piracy has not become a regular habit, although they do chase and rob each other. If you have a chance of watching gulls at a refuse tip or on an estuary where they feed, observe and record carefully examples of piracy. What species are involved? Who chases whom? Is the chase successful? How many birds are involved? What are the ages of the birds? (Careful study of gulls' plumages can help you differentiate juveniles, first winter, second winter, adult – *see* Grant, 1986.) As a bonus you might find a rare gull, such as a ring-billed gull from America, or a glaucous gull from Greenland, or a Mediterranean Gull.

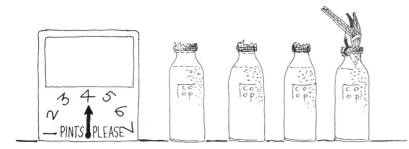

Although tits have traditionally been the milk stealers, we must now beware of the crow family, especially the magpie, and gulls which have developed the habit.

Birds and Berries

Naturalists who watch birds feeding on fruits such as yew, *Cotoneaster*, holly, hawthorn and wild cherry have a good opportunity to discover several things.

The blackbird is a well-watched bird, with at least three books in English and one in German devoted to its life-history. It has several strategies for finding food, depending on the time of year. When the ground is soft enough, it will search for earthworms, or insects in rough grass, but in October and November, above all, it eats berries. At this time of year, in Oxford, Snow (1958) found it was haws.

In my garden in Devon and in several neighbours' gardens a favourite food is rowan berries in September and October – our tree is visited by up to six at a time, and is stripped by as early as the 7th October, always from the top down! Ours is a wild rowan; next door's cultivated variety has redder berries, but is never tackled until ours is nearly empty. In the garden, *Cotoneaster* berries are favourites too, later in the year. *The Birds of the Western Palaearctic* vol. 5 lists haws,

Female blackbird feeding on Cotoneaster berries. She ate seventy-nine berries in thirty minutes.

> ### A FEMALE BLACKBIRD'S MEAL
>
> I watched a female blackbird on 11th November feeding on *Cotoneaster horizontalis* berries from 09.35–10.05: 30 minutes.
>
> 09.35–09.53: ate 67 berries, with long pauses after 31, 42, 55, 67.
> 09.55: ate 6 more while I picked up fallen berries under the bush.
> 10.04–10.05: ate 6 more as I photographed her. Then flew off down the garden.
>
> Total intake: 79 berries
> Weight of 40 berries: 9.5g
> Estimated weight of meal: 18–20g
> Average weight of a female in November: 107g

rowans and *Cotoneaster* (and many other berries) as blackbird food, but does not publish any details of how much food is eaten, save for the fruits of *Prunus mahaleb* in Spain (one observer recording averages of 79 seconds per visit, taking 5.8 fruits per visit and ingesting 5.5 fruits per minute).

Other garden birds that can be watched closely, feeding on seeds, are bullfinches feeding on seed capsules of the violet (nibbling and chewing one after the

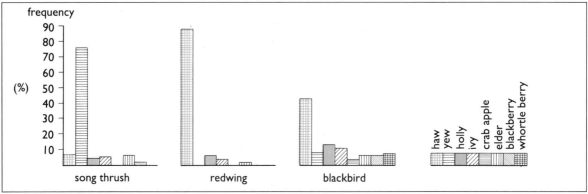

Comparative frequencies of records of the plucking of certain wild fruits by blackbird, song thrush and redwing. For each species of bird the relative frequencies of the fruits they ate are shown as percentages of the total number of fruits consumed (Hartley, 1954).

Some birds find nourishment in the seed, while others are more interested in the pulp (pericarp). In autumn, blackbird and blackcap droppings are stained bluish-purple, a sure sign that they have been eating blackberries. The seeds are not digested and pass straight through the birds' digestive system. Greenfinches on the other hand, rip *Cotoneaster* berries to pieces, drop the yellow-lined red shell and eat the seeds.

SIX THINGS TO DO

1. List the species that feed on berries. Note the comparative abundance of the birds. Are any berries favourites of any particular species?

2. Weigh a number of berries. Calculate the average weight of one. Count the number of berries eaten by one bird and then calculate the weight of food eaten at a sitting. You will need a laboratory balance or ringer's balance weighing in 0.5g divisions at least.

other for five minutes is my record), and goldfinches on dandelion heads. Once, in ten minutes, I watched an adult male goldfinch choose five closed heads one after the other. It grasped the stem with one foot (*see* Project 31), 'walked' the stem down until it lay on the grass then ate every seed of the 'clock'. It flew off after that.

3. Does a goldfinch nibbling dandelion clocks work harder to get enough food, compared with a blackbird picking rowan berries?

4. Try to discover what enables a bird to judge whether it has found good food or not: sight, feel, taste? Attempt to work this out by putting harmless imitation berries on a fruiting bush, and studying the birds' reactions. Or put the imitation berries on the bird-table.

The imitation fruits can be differently coloured raisins and sultanas painted with a thick suspension of watercolour paint. Others could be made of seeds moulded into a fatty ball, and coloured with food colouring.

5. To test the palatability of small wild seeds and grains is more difficult. Collect identified seeds such as fat hen, species of sorrel, wild carrot, hedge parsley or other umbellifers, or red campion. All these plants drop many seeds naturally.

Put a known number or weight of one sort on a tin lid. Place several different lids of seeds at the feeding station. You will need to encourage feeders first by baiting the lids with the successful wild-bird seed you usually buy.

6. If a horse-chestnut tree grows near you study it carefully. Do any birds eat or attempt to eat the nuts or 'conkers'? Are the conker cases impregnable? Do any birds peck and manage to break fallen conkers? Do any birds bury or hide them? At present we know very little in answer to any of these questions.

Fieldfares feeding on ornamental crab apple (Malus) fruit in a suburban garden during cold weather in February.

Pellets

Many species of birds cough up pellets of undigested food, which can then be analysed to discover what the birds have been eating recently.

It is well known that birds of prey eject pellets of indigestible material. These have been collected and analysed, especially for such birds as owls, kestrel and buzzard, and reveal what vertebrates and insects (especially beetles) have been eaten. The vertebrates are revealed by bones, fur and feathers; the hard, chitinous elytra (wing cases) of beetles often almost wholly form the pellets of little owls. Unfortunately, although many other species cough up pellets, they are either difficult to collect or do not give a fair idea of the birds' diet because the species eat foods (like fish) which are almost completely digested. I have seen robin, magpie, blackbird and spotted flycatcher eject pellets but only the blackbird and magpie pellets could be found – the former made of blackberry pips, and the latter mostly of gravel. Crow, gull and heron pellets are quite easy to find at roosts or near a nest site. Many owl and hawk pellets are similarly easily collected. Although analysis of these pellets may not reveal all about a bird's diet, it will provide material which, when backed up by field observations, may give a thorough enough appraisal of it. Field observations at close quarters may be improved by using a hide at a nestbox such as the one shown in Project 6 (*see* page 22), or by using photography.

Authorities differ as to the best way to dissect pellets. Most soak the pellets, which then disintegrate easily and, once dried (over blotting paper, for example), can be studied and the remains identified. Alternatively, the dry pellets may be carefully picked to pieces. One must work very slowly and gently because many of the remains to be identified are small and fragile. A good magnifying glass is an essential aid, and a microscope must be used if such things as small insect parts and earthworm chaetae are to be traced. Analysis of one sample will not show that species' diet, but only something of what it has been eating at that time and place. A thousand or more pellets, collected in every season, may have to be analysed before it is possible to obtain any 'results' that can be taken as full or conclusive. If you wish to keep the dissected contents of the

COMMON PREY ITEMS IN OWL PELLETS	
Small bird	1 unit
Voles	1 unit
Common shrew	0.5 unit
Water shrew	0.75 unit
Pygmy shrew	0.25 unit
Frog	1 unit
Rat	5 units
Beetles	0.05 unit

pellets, mount the items on stiff white card, (saved from a shirt packet or the back of a cereal box). Use a clear adhesive. Keep the mounted specimens in a clear plastic bag containing some insecticide to deter moths and mites.

An interesting review of the results obtained from the analysis of pellets of several species of owls may be found in Sparks and Soper (1970) and *The Birds of the Western Palaearctic* vol. 4.

A survey in Devon found that on average, by weight, the barn owls' food was approximately 60.4 per cent voles, 20.3 per cent mice and 17.8 per cent shrews. A reasonable way of judging how much food of a certain kind the owls have eaten is to use HN Southern's 'prey-unit' system which he pioneered when studying tawny owls. A vole weighs one unit. On average a common shrew is only half as heavy, so he weighs half a unit. The table above shows the comparative weights of the common prey likely to be found in owl pellets, expressed as 'prey units'.

As an aid to mammal identification, the diagrams on the lsft are included. However, the keen pellet investigator will need, in addition, a copy of the Mammal Society's identification booklet (for address *see* page 125).

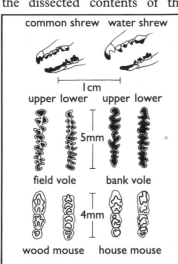

Teeth patterns of six mammals commonly found as prey items.

PROJECT 29

ANALYSIS OF PELLETS OF A GREAT GREY SHRIKE

Date	Place	No. of pellets	Contents
1 April 1971	Horrabridge, Devon	15 or 16 (several broken so difficult to judge)	60% insect remains, including dor beetles and three-horned dor beetles. 40% fur and bones of short-tailed vole.
5 April 1971	Horrabridge Devon	at least 30	30% insect remains. 70% fur and bones of short-tailed vole and upper jaw of a common shrew.

(Data from A Giamosso.)

It has been shown that 'bird = 1 unit' is rather inaccurate; a more accurate way to assess the probable weight of bird prey caught by owls is by showing the relationship of the bird's weight to the length of the humerus.

Anyone fortunate enough to be able to watch a red-backed or great grey shrike may be able to collect and analyse its pellets. Alternatively, a study may be made of the shrike's strange habit of impaling food on thorns, the so-called 'shrike's larder', which is still not fully understood.

Recently, scientists have discovered that laboratory studies of birds' droppings (faeces) have revealed data about prey species and diet generally, which had hitherto been guessed at, or had been known only by the dissection of stomach contents.

Waders, in particular, have been studied by analysing faeces, and results have been published for dunlin, grey plover and green sandpiper, for example (*see* below left). Samples can be preserved in 70 per cent ethanol. In the laboratory the aggregated solids are then separated (deflocculated) for eight to twelve hours in 2M sodium hydroxide before being examined under a microscope of between 12x and 100x magnification. Prey items can then be identified usually to the family at least, by spotting insect mouthparts, mollusc fragments, the chaetae of worms, and the jaws of ragworms, *Nereis spp*. (Barrett and Yonge, 1958, have clear diagrams of their mouthparts). A good description of these methods can be found in Ormerod and Tyler (1988).

DIET OF GREEN SANDPIPERS WINTERING IN SOUTH WALES

	1986	1987
Crustaceans	0.2	1.2
Mayfly nymphs	95.7	90.9
Stonefly nymphs	1.8	0.5
Caddis larvae	1.8	4.2
Truefly larvae	0.5	3.25

(From Ormerod and Tyler, 1988, showing percentages of prey items.)

The barn owl is one of the most studied birds which coughs up pellets.

PROJECT 30

Wormdiggers, Nutcrackers and Shellsmashers

The differently shaped bills of birds are for searching out and eating different foods. It is fascinating to watch closely not only what a bird eats but how it eats.

In 1973, in this book's first edition I wrote, 'so perhaps it will not be long before someone experiments to see what happens when a curlew or a godwit probes in mud ... '. Thirteen years later came the answer: the curlew's bill is adapted to a technique of prey capture in which the bill tip follows a complex three-dimensional search path and the long bill of the common curlew is adapted to the intact removal of long prey (for example, worms) from the mudflats, and is a better instrument than a bar-tailed godwit's. That discovery, described in Davidson *et al.* (1986), was the result of years of careful observation and complicated analysis of the measurements of the two species. But there are simpler ways to begin to learn about a bird's feeding habits.

Take the blackbird for example. Although its diet is well known, as shown in the reference books, you do not know if your blackbirds conform.

TO SHOW HOW A BIRD'S FEEDING HABITS CHANGE DURING THE YEAR

- Choose a study area with good visibility.
- Several times a month make a round of the study area.
- Note exactly where each bird was feeding.
- Try to record every bird in the area.
- Compare your records with those of other workers.

One good study area is a wood; another is a lake and its shore. It is easy to think of a wood as a wood: just trees. And birds in a wood are just in a wood. But in recent years, some consideration has been given to the precise part of the wood that certain species usually inhabit, and this is worth further investigation. Tits have been found to have a preference for a certain height in the trees when feeding. Thus there is a vertical zonal distribution of the species, which helps to counteract specific competition. With tits there is also a horizontal zoning because different species choose to feed close to or away from the trunk along a fir branch.

A wood can be conveniently divided vertically into five divisions: (a) the canopy, that is the topmost branches of the trees, (b) the main part of the trees, (c) the lower branches and shrub layer, (d) the field layer, and (e) the ground (*see also* page 66). It will be noticed that in sessile oak and beechwood, zone (c) may not exist.

The blackbird deserves further detailed study; although a ground feeder mostly, it does take fruit still on trees. How high will it usually go for it: ivy berries, cherries, haws? I have watched juvenile and adult blackbirds in the canopy day after day feeding on wild cherries. Other suitable subjects throughout the year would be the robin, chaffinch, greenfinch and goldcrest (*see also* Project 34).

A lake will also be found to be invisibly divided by the birds that use it. Why do some never venture far from shore? Why are others always seen in open water?

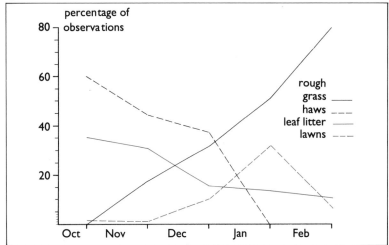

The changes in the feeding habits of the blackbird through the winter (Snow, 1958.)

58

PROJECT 30

PLACE			DATE		TIME
Species	**Activity**				
	Feeding on land	Surface feeding	Head under	Up ending	Preening	Roosting
Mallard						
Tufted duck						
Coot						
Canada goose						
Great crested grebe						
Moorhen						
etc.						

Duplicate a batch of sheets, each one for a different place and/or time period. Analysis could be revealing.

Try completing the table above, ticking each record (in say, a ten-minute period) in each box:

A bird's diet is the list of all it eats, how much it eats and when it eats. Such studies are rare and are usually the work of someone who has for some reason or other fallen in love with a species, and has devoted years to its study. Mountfort (1957) explains in his chapter 'The hawfinch's diet' that the work was based on 'more than five hundred different observations of feeding hawfinches, all but thirty of which are from my own records ... No claim is made that the analysis is complete ... and the observations are spread over a number of years in a number of different countries.'

The hawfinch can crack a cherry stone, exerting with its beak a crushing load varying from 27 to 43kg (60 to 95lb). I was even more intrigued watching hawfinches nibble hornbeam seeds, manipulate them into a certain unknown position, and crack them, with a sound audible at about 9m (30 ft). Although I have tried, I have never succeeded in cracking open a hornbeam seed (I have crushed many), yet hawfinches strew the woodland floor with perfectly split halves. Mountfort's analysis of the species' diet is a fine yardstick for any ornithologist who wishes to copy his example.

Two common birds whose feeding habits are intriguing are the carrion crow and the herring gull. Both gather shellfish on the seashore, carry the mussel or cockle to a height and then drop it, thus hoping to break open the shell to get at the flesh. How widespread is the habit? How many individuals do it? What ground do they choose? How successful are they? How many drops are needed to give a broken shell? How high do the birds fly before dropping a shell? How successful are they compared with oystercatchers which can and do regularly feed on shellfish?

Snail shells littering the turf beside a stone are a sure sign of a song thrush's anvil. How long does a thrush use a favourite stone?

Right- or Left-Footed

We are all very familiar with the fact that some people are left-handed, but most of us are right-handed. Is the same true among birds?

Being left-handed as a person can be most inconvenient. Manufacturers are slow to be helpful by providing left-handed potato peelers or left-handed hockey sticks! I once watched a Kestrel that proved to be repeatedly left-handed or rather left-footed!

Footedness in birds is not well documented. There is some evidence of it in domestic pigeons, which tend to be right-footed. The crossbill's bill has the tips of the mandible crossed to help it extract seeds from fir cones. If the lower mandible crosses to the right, the bird holds the cone in the left foot, and vice versa. By this means it is better able to extract a seed from between the cone's scales.

Many other birds use their feet to help them eat a meal: tits, crows, birds of prey, siskin, goldfinch and nuthatch. It will be some time before you gather enough information to make an analysis but by then you may well have seen enough to make it well worth publishing. Keeping a record will help (*see* panel).

Such a list could easily be stored on a computer database until it gave enough data to be analysed. Try watching coal tits at first, especially those that steal a peanut from the bird-table.

One kestrel has been observed to feed using its left foot. Is your local Kestrel left- or right-footed? This one is a male.

A LEFT-FOOTED KESTREL

On the 14th August, a male was perched on an oak, looking alertly to and fro onto a slope facing his perch. Three times during the morning I saw him return to his perch with food. Between 09.30 and 11.15 on the 15th, he made five kills. It was tantalizingly difficult to see the prey, but on one occasion, I saw him shred (or skin) it and then swallow the rest whole.

As the days went by, I saw a bit more and I feel confident he was eating black slugs (probably *Arion ater*). Each one was held in the left foot; the slug was ripped with his bill until skinned, then swallowed whole. That always left him with a shiny, dirty left foot (quite noticeable beside the shiny yellow right toes), which he always carefully cleaned with his bill before roosting or hunting. I only once saw him work 'right-footed'.

EXAMPLES OF THE HANDEDNESS OF SOME DIFFERENT SPECIES

Species	Date	Place	Left	Right	Prey	Length of time	Perched, on ground or flying
Kestrel	16/08	Home	x		slug	2 min	perched
Osprey	12/04	Majorca	x		fish	30 min	perched
Coal tit	01/01	Home		x	sun-flower	1 min	perched
Hobby	20/06	Dartmoor		x	dragonfly	1 min	flying

Tool Users

One of the strangest and least-known aspects of feeding behaviour among birds is the rare use of tools to help obtain food.

Very few birds use tools, at least, that is what we used to think. Using a tool means picking up an object and using that to aid one's purpose, such as picking up or reaching food. In the animal kingdom it is usually considered to be an instinctive behaviour or the result of a simple learning process and not a sign of great intelligence. The tool-using bird, for example, is simply fulfilling a need; it does not think ahead, like a human, and invent a tool to serve a particular purpose. There is some scientific argument about the precise definition of tool-using, but few would disagree that, as far as birds are concerned, it means picking up an inanimate object and using it by holding it in its bill or foot to perform a task.

It is quite likely that British birds other than those in the panel are waiting to be recorded. Our herons, nuthatches and members of the crow family have similar habits to their American counterparts (*see* panel); their instinctive behaviour in looking for food could lead them to use a tool by chance one day, learn its effectiveness and so do it again (and perhaps have others learn from them). If one tit can use a poking stick, so might others (*see* Project 39).

Two tool users. The woodpecker finch uses a twig or cactus spine to prise grubs from holes in a tree and the Egyptian vulture hurls stones to break egg shells that it cannot crack with its bill.

KNOWN TOOL-USERS

Woodpecker finches of the Galapagos Islands use a cactus spine to prise out insects from crevices.

Black-breasted kites of Australia and *Egyptian Vultures* in Africa drop stones on emu and ostrich eggs respectively in order to break the shells and eat the contents.

Green herons in North America have been seen repeatedly using fish-food pellets to help catch fish at a seaquarium!

Brown-headed nuthatches in North America sometimes use a flake of bark to lever off another flake to find food.

Blue jays in a North American aviary poked paper through a cage to scoop up food which was otherwise out of reach.

A blackbird in England has once been recorded using an 8cm (3in) twig to clear snow 4–5cm (1.5–2in) deep to an area of about 900cm² (140 in²).

The closely related *American robin* has been seen to use a twig similarly to clear the ground of leaf litter to get at ants.

A blue tit in England was seen to poke a peanut out of a nut hopper, using a twig about 2cm (0.75in) long held in its beak. It took about three minutes to get a nut.

5. BEHAVIOUR

Bird behaviour is a vast, complicated subject which gives a birdwatcher never-ending pleasure, much data to analyse, and argument about interpreting the results!

Previous chapters have already introduced us to several aspects of bird behaviour, in particular how they communicate with each other, find food and rear their young. Away from the garden, as we continue to watch and study 'in the field', we may well become very involved in studying bird flight, courtship, aggression, intelligence, care for their feathers and migration.

One October evening, I was sitting on the shore of an estuary, when over the mudflats flew a herring gull with a small flatfish in its bill. It was pursued by a great black-backed gull. After some yards of mad, twisting flight the fish was dropped. Another herring gull moved in and grabbed it, only to be chased by a second great black-backed gull. Over the mudflats they twisted and turned; a third great black-backed gull joined in, and got the fish when it was again dropped. It swallowed the fish, but was immediately attacked by a fourth great black-backed gull and forced to flee with the attacker in pursuit. The fish was disgorged, and the pursuer successfully retrieved it and appeared to have dominance on the ground over any newcomer. Two black-backs which came near retreated after being threatened. The fish was swallowed again, presumably for good.

Later the same day, on the same shore, I was watching an oystercatcher feeding. After crossing about 45m (50 yds) of shore, its bill was completely covered with mud, having been repeatedly plunged to its base. As soon as it stepped into a freshwater stream which flowed onto the mud, it drank. Next it cleaned its bill, swilled its head, dipped its belly feathers, then sat in the stream, looking like a duck. There it preened its back,

An oystercatcher feeding.

rump and tertial feathers, splashing and wriggling for four minutes, then sat still and soaked, followed by more splashing and preening. Suddenly, it violently flapped its wings, after which it dipped its head and breast repeatedly until, without warning, it walked out of the stream, shook itself, and took off with a 'roar' of wet feathers. It landed near the tideline and preened further, starting with the right wing, walking a few metres as it did so. Finally, after thirteen minutes of preening it flew off, joined three others and resumed feeding.

These two observations are examples of the very fascinating but complicated study of bird behaviour. One was social, the other non-social. Both were concerned with the individuals' survival, the one demonstrated by piratical food-hunting gulls, the other by a wader attending to its plumage, especially its wings, in order to be always in perfect flying condition. The examples reveal that a bird's life is not haphazard: in its world of fast living (flying demands a rapid assimilation and release of energy), its life must be organized; a chaotic, anarchic lack of system would not benefit its survival. A bird's private life is organized so that it looks after itself with habits of feeding, preening, flying and social behaviour which are similar throughout the species, and are best suited to that species' survival.

The social behaviour demands sophisticated communications if individuals of a species are to keep together, especially to satisfy the need for successful reproduction. 'As free as a bird' has little meaning, for a bird's social life is from beginning to end governed by ritualized signals, by action and reaction. Burton's (1985) concise, attractively illustrated summary of this complex subject is compulsory reading, as is Tinbergen's and Falkus's (1970) book, called significantly, *Signals for Survival*. Social behaviour, which depends on signals given and received, is not confined to calls and songs but also to special movements of the wings, head and tail, the use of special adornments, such as a crest or ruff, or brilliant colours.

Armstrong has clearly pointed out what an observer of bird behaviour must do (*see* panel on the right). In addition to notebook records, photographs, films (especially in slow motion) and tape-recordings may be vital evidence in the final analysis.

There can be no doubt that there will be many devoted students in the future who will be prepared to live rough like many of the film-makers who provide wonderful films for television; or like Bryan and June Nelson who lived like Adam and Eve on uninhabited Tower and Hood Islands in the Galapagos. They stayed there a year to study bird behaviour, especially that of boobies (Nelson, 1968), and their self-imposed exile is

The large bustards have exotic courtship. This male little bustard's wing flicking display is no exception.

an adventurous example of the lengths to which bird-watchers will go to study.

WHAT TO DO WHEN OBSERVING A BIRD

- Describe what is seen so that the account can be compared in detail with the displays of other species.
- Similarly, realizing that display is essentially a signalling code, record not only the type of posturing performed by a bird, but its place in a sequence and the reaction of the bird perceiving it. Thirdly, consider of what components a display is composed.
- The observer must be candid and unprejudiced.
- The observer of the display should try and identify its sources and constituents but caution is necessary in reaching conclusions.

Jizz

Watch carefully birds in flight. It will sharpen your powers of observation and improve your ability to identify birds by their characteristic movements and appearance.

Norman MacCaig, the Scottish poet, has recorded a novel experience in one of his poems. Most poets have extolled the skylark's song, but MacCaig was intrigued by its flight:

Lark drives invisible pitons in the air
And hauls itself up the face of space.

In the same poem, *Movements*, he also observes 'swans undulate through clouds', 'a bomb of grouse', a gannet diving like 'a white anchor falling' and 'when it lands/Umbrella heron becomes walking stick'. The poet can teach many a birdwatcher a thing or two, who finds it hard to find the words to describe how a bird moves. For most species of birds, flying is a basic aspect of behaviour and so it is of great interest to notice how differently one species moves and flies compared with another. Each species is adapted to live in its own particular way. The conscious effort of carefully watching a bird's actions will sharpen our powers of observation and will greatly improve our ability to identify many species in a second or so by their characteristic flight pattern and

Common terns fishing in shallow water off a sandy shore.

BIRDS IN FLIGHT

- A *peregrine* is flying at over 100mph (161kph) in a dive.
- A *barn owl* in slow, flapping flight, hunting, is doing only a tenth of the falcon's speed.
- Ducks are fast in level flight: an *eider* has been clocked at 47mph (76kph).
- Miraculously, large flocks of waders like *knot* and *dunlin* all seem to turn together without crashing.
- *Razorbills* and *guillemots* 'fly' underwater, using their wings to swim with, but *cormorants* and *ducks* paddle, using their feet.
- A *dipper* sometimes walks on the river bed; sometimes it 'flies' underwater!

Page from a typical field guide showing a variety of passerines. In more comprehensive guides, juvenile plumages and birds in flight are also shown.

movement, their 'jizz' as it is called. If you learn to recognize the local birds and can, in a moment, be sure of what you have seen when 'something strange is in the air' this can be realized immediately and carefully recorded. It might be an unusual piece of behaviour from a well-known bird, or a glimpse of a bird with which you are not familiar and need to follow or search for in order to identify it.

One never knows what movement it may be that will be worth watching: terns or gannets feeding as if on well-organized bombing raids (*see* Project 35); a swallow's brilliant acrobatic chasing of a feather; the antics of a house sparrow unsuccessfully attacking a dragonfly; a jackdaw trying to catch a falling autumn leaf; black-headed gulls hunting flying ants; a kestrel hovering; several greenshanks running to and fro feeding at the water's edge on a rising tide over a mudflat; a goldcrest looking like a large hoverfly; a chaffinch pretending to be a flycatcher. I have seen all these recently. The jizz of the bird told me that I did have a chaffinch, that the terns were sandwich and not common, and that the goldcrest was worth looking at twice to double check it was not a pallas's warbler.

Just learning from a book the pattern of a bird's plumage is not sufficient. Certain identification depends, too, on an awareness of the subtleties of one bird's shape compared with another, of the way it stands or walks or hops, of its characteristic flight in a flock or on its own. So, once seen and learned, the jizz of different species will always enable you to differentiate between, for example, a passing winter flock of starlings or thrushes, and pipits or finches.

Birds in a Wood

Most of the surface of Great Britain was formerly woodland. Even today, many of our garden birds are really woodland birds and deserve our careful attention.

In prehistoric times, after the last Ice Age about 10,000 years ago, more than half the land area of Britain was covered in forest. Since the time of the New Stone Age, man has cleared about 90 per cent of that forest. However, our 20th century land-based bird-life, has been shaped by those ancient oak forests, the ash of limestone hills, the pine and birch of uplands, and the willows and alders of marshes and river banks.

If a birdwatcher intends to study intensively birds in a 'wood', he does need more exact terms so that his work in one place may be reasonably compared or contrasted with work in another. He would be wise to use the classification and terms given in the panel during all his woodland birds research.

The list on the opposite page showing the relative abundance of birds in a wood is for summer populations. Relatively few bird-watchers study trees in winter. There may be parts of the woods, then, which are apparently devoid of birds; most birds seen may be tits, but these limitations should not stop you. An excellent project would be to follow and attempt to map the movements of a tit flock through a winter wood. Although each species will be keeping to its feeding zone the flock progresses together and each individual will be maintaining its minimum distance (*see* Project 24). How widely does the flock roam? What species are in the flock? What is the relationship between tits and other species? How fast do they travel? How much feeding is going on

WHAT IS IN EACH LINK OF THE THEORETICAL FOOD CHAIN IN YOUR WOOD?

Name the species at each level of the chain:

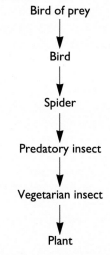

Bird of prey
↓
Bird
↓
Spider
↓
Predatory insect
↓
Vegetarian insect
↓
Plant

Although the idea of food chains is a familiar one to biologists, what *exactly* is in a British woodland chain is not well known and deserves attention.

TERMS AND CLASSIFICATIONS TO USE DURING WOODLAND BIRD RESEARCH

Main types of woodland	Groups of trees	Structure of a tree
broad-leaved woods	wood	trunk
coniferous woods	grove	major branches or limbs
mixed woods	clump	branches
simple coppice	belt	twigs
coppice-with-standards	line	leaves
scrub	stand	flowers
devastated woods	plantation	fruits
felled woods	compartment	
	thicket	
	scrub	
	spinney	
	carr	

For detailed definitions, *see* Simms (1971).

(a) canopy

(b) main tree

(c) shrub

(d) field

(e) ground

Above: *vertical zones in a broad-leaved wood.*
Left: *this beech wood in early spring shows the vertical divisions of this kind of wood.*

compared with storing food? What is the relative abundance of each species in winter? What species have been lost and gained?

A careful reading of two splendid books (*Birds and Woods* by WB Yapp and *Woodland Birds* by Eric Simms) reveals that familiar garden birds such as the chaffinch, robin and blackbird are actually descendents of true woodland species which have adapted to the artificial woodland edge of our shrubs and trees in suburbia. A valuable contribution to our understanding of the lives of our garden birds could be made by comparing the behaviour of one or more of the three species mentioned above in your neighbourhood with the same species living in the natural woodland environment. Are the robins just as tame? Are the blackbirds just as numerous? Do the chaffinches sing more?

Finally, here is another idea to send you into a summer and a winter wood. The woodcock is a secretive species, hard to locate because it is active usually only at dawn and dusk. So, it tends to be under-recorded and its numbers are under-estimated. Our breeding population is augmented by large numbers in winter from Scandinavia. This wader, related to snipe, is adapted to a life probing for food in the soft, damp leaf litter of a wood or plantation. The National Game Census of the Game Conservancy estimates that around 200,000 are shot each year. Hunters know where to find them, but bird-watchers do not search for them or watch these beautiful birds as they do other waders. Your local bird club would welcome a detailed investigation.

RELATIVE ABUNDANCE OF BIRDS IN BRITISH OAK WOODS

Pedunculate oak		Sessile oak	
Chaffinch	13	Chaffinch	17
Robin	11	Pied flycatcher	7
Wren	10	Willow warbler	7
Blackbird	8	Wood warbler	6
Willow warbler	7	Wren	6
Woodpigeon	6	Robin	5
Blue tit	5	Redstart	5
Great tit	4	Tree pipit	5
Garden warbler	3	Coal tit	5
Song thrush	3	Carrion crow	4
Dunnock	2	Woodpigeon	4
Blackcap	2	Blackbird	4
Redstart	1	Great tit	3
Great spotted woodpecker	1	Starling	1

Expressed as a percentage of the total contacts made (Simms 1971).

Seabirds, Shorebirds and Waterbirds

Garden birds are easy to study; woodland birds are easy to find within the finite woodland boundary. Seabirds and other waterbirds are ideal subjects for detailed study, too.

Although there are several splendid books about seabirds, which can help us to identify the auks and gulls and terns, and which illustrate their complicated daily lives, they are no substitute for the real thing. Among the first birds mentioned in English literature are the gannet, a gull and the curlew in the 9th century Anglo-Saxon poem *The Seafarer*. Long before, and ever since, men have not only hunted various seabirds and their eggs for food, but have been fascinated by many aspects of their lives.

The fishing methods of terns are worth studying carefully. Subtle differences in behaviour, as well as plumage and structure, will help you identify little from common from sandwich from black. How much hovering does a tern do? How many dives does it make a minute? How many are successful (the prey is usually in the bill when it flies up again)? Which species fish over open water? Which prefer the shoreline?

Black-headed gulls are common and widespread, especially in autumn and winter. They often work in a loose flock over a given area of water (*see* diagram opposite) and move in a definite pattern, moving up against the wind to an invisible marker, then retreating fast to the end of the queue, and so on up through the feeding area again. The flock will stay over one feeding area for some while. Warm water outfalls at power stations and sewage outlets are favourite spots. A close study of this feeding behaviour might reveal (a) what triggers it, (b) how many birds usually become involved, (c) how often one bird dips for food 'on the beat', (d) what the usual height is, (e) what it is that governs the shape and size of the flock, and (f) what times of day and year are most popular.

A survey in your district of the gulls' habit of following the plough would be worth while. What species are involved? What proportion are immatures? Are they all hunting in the newly turned soil or are some scavenging from successful hunters? (*see also* Project 27). Birdwatchers often watch gulls at rubbish tips, usually in hope of spotting a rarity! Little has been done in studying feeding strategies, and relationships with other gulls and crows.

One of the most interesting sights on the seashore is black-headed gulls on a muddy or sandy shore paddling left-right-left in a pool, as if they were soldiers marking time. The observer would find it instructive to record how many birds are involved, how often, and whether other birds as well as gulls do it. This behaviour is called foot-

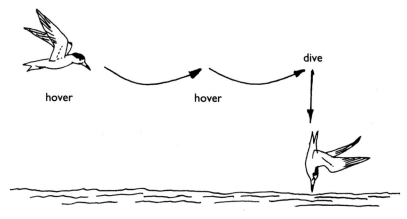

hover   hover   dive

A little tern feeding.

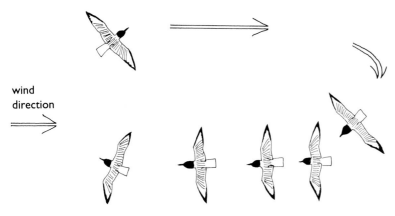

wind
direction

An avocet's upturned bill is specially shaped for sweeping for food in shallow water.

A flock of black-headed gulls feeding.

paddling and clearly it is intended to stir up prey from the mud. It would be of value to try to measure the success of foot-paddling compared with normal searching.

On a nearby shoreline which is often frequented by waders and other birds, try to discover which species favour which zones of the shore. You might be lucky to be able to watch a tideline that regularly has large rafts of beached seaweed. What feeds there? Are the species all waders? Are there any surprises? How long does the seaweed stay? Is it a good source of food? What is the peck-order among the feeding birds?

Wader courtship displays are among the most spectacular of British birds. Waders nest on open shores (oystercatcher and ringed plover), marshes (red-shank and lapwing), and moors (dunlin and golden plover), so cover for the birdwatcher to hide behind is often non-existent. Care must be taken to watch from a distance which does not disturb the birds, or from a hide. Make careful notes of the behaviour of the male and female.

Freshwater habitats are widespread. There is probably a reservoir, flooded gravel pit, canal, river or park lake near you. Because the birds are large compared to garden birds they are easy to see, frequently become tame and so are approachable and easy to study behaving naturally. Waterbirds such as ducks, herons, moorhens and swans are therefore ideal subjects for study.

THROUGH THE YEAR

Birdwatching is an all-the-year-round pastime. Waterbirds are ideal subjects for regular study. Make regular visits to the same area of water.

Moorhens Each month, list and map carefully where they feed: on land, on emergent water-plants, on the water. Note the number of birds; the length of time spent feeding. Record the data in histogram form if you can.

Coots Each month, note carefully the amount of time spent resting in a flock; squabbling with other coots; feeding. (How many dives in a given time? How much dabbling?)

Mallard Month by month, compare the activities of ducks and drakes. How long is the drake 'in eclipse' (in moult plumage)? How much feeding is surface feeding compared with dabbling?

Feather Maintenance

A bird's life depends on its feathers being in perfect condition for insulation, waterproofing and efficient flight. To ensure this is so, a variety of instinctive actions are performed.

A LIST OF ACTIVITIES INVOLVED IN FEATHER MAINTENANCE

The first four are the bird's main activities

- **Bathing** That is true bathing in water. Is it always fresh water and not salt water?
- **Drying** Do not confuse these movements after rain with bathing.
- **Oiling** With oil from the oil gland.
- **Preening** That is combing feathers with bill.
- **Head scratching** With one foot.
- **Sunning*** Sometimes called sunbathing.
- **Dusting*** and dust-bathing.
- **Anting*** (see panel).
- **Comfort movements** That is stretching limbs or ruffling feathers.
- **Care of soft parts** (legs, feet, bill).
- **Smoke bathing***.

* The precise functions of these activities are far from certain and deserve much careful attention.

Birds are vulnerable to predators when preening, so most birds will frequently spend the lengthy period of combing their feathers somewhere under cover, and therefore, unfortunately, hidden from easy observation. But bathing in water by starlings and dust-bathing by house sparrows can be more readily observed and their frequency recorded. Even gulls that may have been swimming on and off during the day in an estuary will readily bathe in fresh water at the head of the estuary at low tide, or in nearby rainwater pools on grassland (such as flooded playing fields). Some scientists believe that besides helping condition the feathers, the freshwater bathing is just a pleasurable experience for the gulls.

Sunbathing, perhaps, serves the same double purpose. Starlings regularly indulge in communal water-bathing. A record of which species bathe and how much they bathe would be worthwhile. How long do the birds take to dry out? Starlings, especially, bathe even in winter and sometimes are stimulated to bathe in seemingly unsuitable cold or rainy conditions.

No birds are more spectacular when drying out than cormorants and shags. How long do they need to dry their wings after a swim?

Perhaps the most extraordinary form of feather care is known as 'anting'. A bird may pick up an ant (or sometimes ants) and stroke its feathers, especially the tail and the wings, presumably to wipe formic acid on them: this is known as 'active anting'. The birds usually ant rapidly with great concentration for several minutes. Anting is an instinctive behaviour pattern because even juveniles do it. A few species have been watched 'passive anting', that is crouching and allowing ants to run over the feathers.

BRITISH SPECIES THAT ANT IN THE WILD

Active anting:
Raven, carrion crow, rook, magpie, jay, chaffinch, house sparrow, mistle thrush, song thrush, blackbird. Green woodpeckers often eat ants but are not certainly known to go anting.

Active and rarely passive anting:
Starling.

The behaviour is apparently confined among European birds to these families: crows, starlings, finches, thrushes and weavers (sparrows). It is possible that anting is related to the emergence of new feathers and the subsequent skin irritation. My own observations have all been in the late summer and autumn (moulting time).

To assist scientists who might analyse future records, your account should include information on (a) the condition of the plumage, (b) the age of the bird, if it can be told from its plumage, (c) the meteorological data for the day of observation and the preceding several days, (d) the number of birds involved, (e) the birds that were not anting but were feeding, and (f) the reactions of birds which were more intent on avoiding the ants. Particularly useful information can be gathered on this unusual behaviour by watching carefully a colony of ants that are easily seen such as those of the wood ant.

Tameness

Scientists who have studied great tits, crows and geese have shown what valuable knowledge about bird behaviour and intelligence can be obtained by studying wild birds that have become tame.

It is an exciting experience, gained by great patience, to get a robin to feed from the hand. Methods of achieving success are no doubt legion, but one that regularly works is to place the food gradually nearer and nearer the observer. Eventually the last meal is on the hand. Do not be afraid of quietly talking to or calling the bird. Many individuals will get to know your voice and come when they hear it. Slow, steady movements and much stillness will get the bird used to you, but much time and patience will be needed before you successfully accomplish this project.

As Lord Percy has put it, 'The one certain passport to their confidence is to induce [the birds] to regard man as a supplier of their favourite food'. So, wheatears, robins and other members of the thrush family may be tempted by mealworms; tits and nuthatches are much attracted to peanuts and sunflower seeds; finches will come to mixed seed. If you bait a particular site in a hedge or a wood (an open patch of ground or a tree stump), test the time the bait takes to be found; list and count the birds that come; and compare the visitors with those at your garden table.

Up and down the land, chaffinches are now a feature of our tourist car-parks and picnic sites. The birds are so used to humans that they will perch on cars in anticipation of a handout. I have watched them thus feeding in Dartmoor National Park, the Yorkshire Dales, Northumberland, South Wales and on the Isle of Mull. Elsewhere, house sparrows are one's picnic companions. How many birds are involved? What times of year? What times of the day do they come? Are they just weekenders appearing when the humans crowd in, or will just a couple of people attract the birds?

Right: at picnic spots, birds such as this female house sparrow become extremely tame and regularly come to the hand to take scraps of food.
Below: *these shags are drying their wings after fishing. Both shags and cormorants must do this because their feathers are not as waterproof as those of other waterfowl.*

Migration

Although from ancient times mankind has been fascinated by the regular comings and goings of many birds, there is still much we can learn.

In the Bible, in the *Book of Jeremiah*, we read that 'Even the stork in the heavens knows her times, and the turtledove, swallow and crane keep the time of their coming'. That was written in about 600BC, making it one of the oldest written accounts of migrants we have. The miracle of migration is still as striking to us today as it was to the prophet.

'One swallow does not make a summer', but it is a powerful reminder of the miracle of migration. If the observer keeps a careful note, for each regular migrant in his experience, of the first arrival and the last seen, he will store up a wealth of information that will enable him to become familiar with something of the migration patterns of birds such as warblers, swallows, waders and wildfowl. The simplest variation of this project is to try to see an earlier or a later bird of a species than you have ever seen before. I am still excited by an April swift, or an October flycatcher, or, best of all, by the first willow warbler I hear singing each year. Knowledge of the usual arrival and departure dates in your area will help you judge the importance of an unusual passage of migrants.

Two forms of migration are particularly exciting: firstly, cold weather movements, when birds are driven, often in large numbers, by bad weather to seek more hospitable territory – birds such as redwings, fieldfares, skylarks and lapwings; secondly, certain species are known to erupt from their normal breeding range overseas in times of food shortage. So, the British Isles and North America are periodically invaded by waxwings, crossbills and nutcrackers from the northern forests. All observations of cold weather movements and irruptions should be sent to the local county birdwatching society to build as complete a picture of the movements as possible.

One of the best ways of observing migration is to visit, or better still stay at, the nearest bird observatory in spring or autumn. This may be based at a specially built observatory, as at the world-famous Fair Isle Observatory between the Orkneys and Shetlands, north of Scotland. Others may be in a caravan, cottage, old lighthouse or log cabin; it all depends on what the local bird club can afford. But whatever the accommodation, the observatory is there because it is on a known flight-path. Failing that, visit regularly a north- or south-facing headland or a pass between hills to look for newly arrived migrants. Observatories are administered by independent committees (addresses are given on page 125).

If you live near a lighthouse, it might be worth a visit (with permission) because migrants are attracted to the light, often with sadly disastrous results. The death toll, when noted, can be

Map of Britain and Ireland showing the positions of the major bird observatories. Accommodation is available at most of them. Full addresses are given on page 125.

SOME MIGRANTS TO EXCITE YOU AT THE WRONG TIME OF YEAR

Common Sandpiper
Normally seen on spring and autumn passage, but 100 or so winter on ponds, lakes and estuaries in Britain, the extreme northern edge of its wintering range. Study one carefully. Is it a common or a very similar North American spotted sandpiper? How long does it stay? What is the size of its territory?

Cuckoo Its call is so easily imitated that a sight record is essential if you wish to convince your county recorder that you have recorded one in March, or even early April.

Chiffchaff This bird usually winters in the Mediterranean region and West Africa. Yet each year, several hundreds are recorded wintering especially in south and west Britain.

Fieldfare and redwing We usually think of these thrushes as autumn and winter visitors, but if you live in northern Britain look out for them in the breeding season. Fieldfares first nested in Britain in 1967 and redwings in 1925. Both are afforded special protection.

Blackcap They have increased in numbers over the past fifteen years in winter, coming more and more commonly to our gardens and bird tables instead of wintering in southern Europe or North Africa. What do they feed on? Ringing returns have shown they are from breeding populations in central Europe, not British birds.

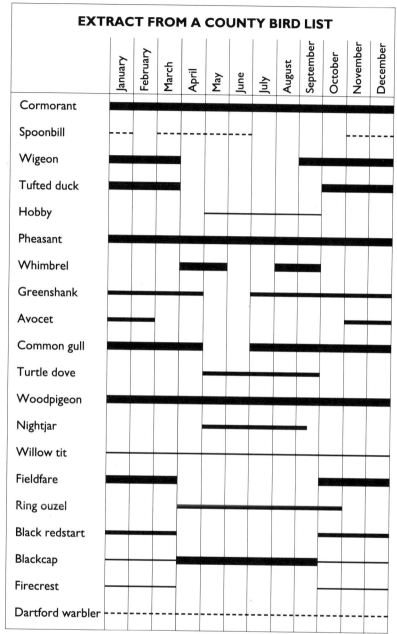

EXTRACT FROM A COUNTY BIRD LIST

These examples from a county bird list show how different species are present at different times of the year. Thick lines (▬) indicate that a species can be found on most visits to the appropriate habitat at the correct time of year. Lines of medium thickness (▬) represent less common species and thin lines (—) indicate species that are infrequently seen. A dashed line (---) is for a species rarely seen. A good project is to construct such a chart for your local birds.

used as a sample to illustrate what is migrating, when, and in what strength. In the United States, in Kansas and in Florida, scientists have studied the specimens killed in poor weather in collision with television aerial towers. As the number of towers increases, observation and collection of specimens will certainly yield additional information about nocturnal migration.

Intelligence Tests

Bird behaviour may be divided into instinctive and learned. How much the latter is due to refining the former is a moot point.

A young bird does not have to learn how to fly. Its survival demands that it does, instinctively. However, each bird does gain prowess in the air by learning to perform manoeuvres, such as turning and landing, more and more skillfully.

How much of birds' behaviour is owed to intelligence? How far do they react to given stimuli? A blue tit *learns* how to open a milk bottle (*see* Project 27), using instinctive pecking actions it would use on tree bark or a beech nut. Intelligence does not lead it to think 'Ah, there is food in this bottle if I can open the lid!' Intelligence is shown if we can observe an individual often enough and realize that its actions are not just instinctive or learned but show anticipation, which is sure evidence that the bird is thinking.

The garden birdwatcher has probably one of the best opportunities for judging for himself whether garden birds are intelligent. The simplest test is to tie a peanut to the end of a piece of

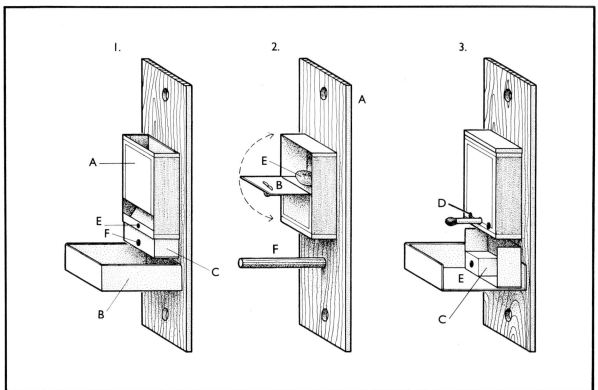

Three types of matchbox apparatus which can be used in intelligence tests with tits. In each case a matchbox case (A) is glued to a stout card or piece of wood that can be pinned to a tree or fence. In (1), part of the front is cut away to let the peanut fall into the matchbox drawer (B) when the bird taps down the inner box (C) from the top. C consists of another drawer and a piece of bent card (D) which closes the opening when the apparatus is set. The test can be modified by inserting a match in holes E and F which are in the case and box respectively. The bird then has to remove the match first.

In (2), the upper half of the front of the matchbox (B) is cut and hinged, and is weighted (C) so that it drops open when released. A top (D) is fixed on the box; this has a small fold along its front edge to hold the door shut until the bird pulls at the weight and so exposes the nut on a shelf (E). A perch (F) is added.

In (3), a matchbox drawer (B) is cut to half-length, weighted and made to move easily in its case, which again has a top. It is provided with a socket (C), so that a matchstick through a hole (D) in the case locks the drawer until pulled out, whereupon B falls into the tray (E) exposing the nut. Other holes level with D are dummies so that the tit can be confronted with three sticks.

string so that birds can reach it only by perching at the top of the string and pulling it up. Tits can perform quite complicated tricks and solve intricate puzzles. Perhaps the most strange one known is the actions performed by tame varied tits in Japan, which on the command of their masters at a fair, will take your money, open a box and take out your fortune printed on a slip of paper. In Britain, blue and coal tits seem best at solving puzzles.

INTELLIGENCE TESTS

Intelligence tests for tits were devised by Brooks-King and Hurrell (1958). Basically, the idea is to offer peanuts to tits in puzzle boxes, from which the nut cannot be extracted without the correct solution to the problem. The puzzle box is shown with various adaptations in the diagram on the previous page.

It is certain from experiments made so far that some species seem cleverer than others, that certain individual birds are more able than others, and that those who do 'pass' a test do not forget how to do it again

Most tests that I know of expect tits to be participants; and they all depend on food for bait. Can you devise a test for ground-feeding dunnocks? Mine are so 'dozy' they will not go to a wire-box chardonneret trap with the lid at the top, which I use for trapping and ringing tits and finches. They walk round and round, seeing the food beyond the wire, but never flying up to the door at the top of the cage.

The most unusual species that I know whose intelligence has been tested is the water rail. This is normally a shy and secretive bird of reedbeds and lake margins. Lord William Percy (1951) watched, photographed and tested one from a hide (*see* diagram below). After a few hours it could jump up to get a worm impaled on the end of a reed. That was a really wild bird, unaffected by the gadgets and feeding stations in a birdwatcher's garden. If a so-called shy, skulking bird like the water rail can be such a good participant, who knows what else might be put to the test and what they could achieve.

Lord Percy's test on a water rail.

Courtship Displays

The survival of the species depends on successful mating and raising a brood to fledging. Courtship displays are a vital part of this.

In spring, in the garden, you may become aware that three birds are chasing each other through the shrubbery. They land among the open, leafless branches of a pussy willow and you see that they are dunnocks, two of which are calling excitedly and fanning their wings above their backs. Suddenly, all three are off again, zig-zagging through the bushes and out of sight into the next-door garden. Later, the blue tit, which had obviously taken over the nest box in the New Year, leaves his perch and crosses the garden with a few slow wing-beats, and a short glide with wings spread wide, looking more like a large green and blue butterfly than a bird.

Once you become aware of this apparently exceptional behaviour you will have entered the world of sexual displays, many of which are even more fascinating to watch and study than the two described above. Indeed, the dull, dun-coloured dunnock leads an extraordinary life, a fact which has only recently been described. A female may mate with only one male (a monogamous mating), but if her feeding territory meets two males' territories she may well mate with both (a polyandrous mating). Among other passerines (perching birds or songbirds are the popular descriptions of this, the largest classification of birds), too many males in an area means some will

SPECIES THAT MAY GIVE YOU SOME SURPRISES

Even though amateur and professional birdwatchers have filled volumes about the lives of British birds, some species which are common and/or widespread have not been studied extensively. Careful observation over the course of several seasons could be very revealing. Here are some suggestions in alphabetical order:

Bullfinch
Common sandpiper
Garden warbler
Goldcrest
Long-tailed tit
Magpie
Meadow pipit
Rock pipit
Song thrush
Stock dove
Water rail
Wood warbler

not get a mate. But dunnocks have evolved a strategy that ensures females get a mate, all males have a chance to mate, and females may well have two mates to help rear the brood.

Since this has been discovered only recently, one wonders what other fascinating life stories are hidden in our woods, gardens and reedbeds.

ASPECTS WORTHY OF STUDY

Certain aspects of sexual display are particularly worthy of study:

1. Aerial displays and song flights are probably commoner than realized. Of particular interest are: (a) the relationship of display to territoriality and the

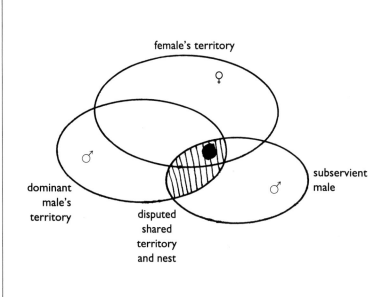

Diagram of dunnocks' territories. This female has mated with two males who have adjoining territories. Her territory overlaps with each of theirs and the nest has been built in the area where all three territories overlap.

female (*see* Project 12); (b) the frequency and seasonal incidence of display flights; (c) the relationship between display and colouration, and habitat. Species of particular interest would be larks, pipits, birds of prey, whitethroat, sedge warbler, lapwing, common snipe and greenfinch.

2. Aquatic displays, like aerial ones, cannot be studied well in aviaries, so the field observer has an important rôle to play. Few aquatic displays have been thoroughly studied. A model is that by Simmons (1955) on the great crested grebe.

3. Corporate displays are exciting and much more remains to be understood about even such well-documented displays as those of ruff, sage grouse and blackcock. Easier to find may be shelduck, oystercatcher, lapwing and house sparrow.

4. Pair formation: how does one sex identify the other? What differences are there in display before a first brood and before the second? Does display obey a rhythm and reach peaks at certain times?

5. Greeting: an extensive field for study because there is doubt whether some displays are greeting or appeasement.

6. Courtship feeding: the relationship of ceremonial feeding to normal feeding, and to feeding of young, and the presentation of nest material all deserve study for little is known. Titmice using the nestbox made in Project 5 would make an ideal subject for study. Does the male feed the female, or *vice versa*, or both?

Songs or calls that are associated with displays must be considered as part of the performance. They should not be treated as a separate project.

Only the male ruff develops this impressive collar of feathers during the breeding season. Groups of males display together on areas of ground called leks. Many different patterns of ruff occur.

Aggressive displays

Both male and female birds, at times, are aggressive towards members of their own species and other birds in defence of a food supply or a nest.

Aggressive display, when a bird postures to threaten another, is exciting to watch. I have seen two wrens fall fighting to the road from a bush, feet locked together; I walked to within a few feet of them before they flew away. Most birds, however, threaten others of the species by special postures and calls and rarely does injury or death occur: that would hardly benefit either individual in the fight. There follow seven particular lines of research you may like to pursue.

1. Watch a common species such as a robin or blackbird, carefully note the displays, compare notes with an authority (Cramp 1988) and so identify the aggressive displays.

2. Make a study of the behaviour of birds towards predators. Encounters of this kind are usually witnessed by chance and so notes accumulate only over a number of years. The investigation might analyse (a) the bird and animal species most frequently mobbed; (b) the birds that most often mob the predators; then (c) a comparison of mobbing in open country with mobbing in woodland; and (d) some species will mob alone, for example a carrion crow against a hawk, but others usually flock before they threaten (for example swallows against a kestrel). This particular aspect of behaviour is worth careful attention and observation..

3. Aggressive display by various species against stuffed birds such as owls and cuckoos, and even their own reflections, has been well documented by Smith and Hosking (1955). These investigators studied reactions at nests. This would now be unlawful without a permit (*see* page 19), but similar experiments using stuffed predators, portions of predators (what part of a hunter makes a bird mad?), cutouts or models might well be done at the bird table, although the drive to defend and attack will of course be less than at the nest. The interest would lie in (a) which birds reacted most violently; (b) what caused the aggressive reaction; and (c) precisely how did they react?

Smith and Hosking found the reactions shown in the panel

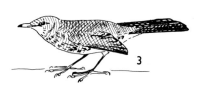

Aggressive postures of a fieldfare watched with other thrushes feeding in winter on fallen apples in an old orchard. (1) mild threat; (2) intense threat display which was often followed by (3), a crouching run at the 'enemy' redwing, blackbird or fieldfare.

REACTIONS OF WILLOW WARBLERS TO STUFFED DUMMIES

Dummy	Reaction
1. Sectional cuckoo with tail and wings only	medium fear: *hewie* note
2. Sectional cuckoo with tail, wings and head	aggressive reaction: chittering note and attack
3. Whole cuckoo	violent, aggressive chittering note and attack on dummy held in hand
4. Hen sparrowhawk	strong fear reaction: *hewie* note
5. Red-footed falcon	aggressive chittering note and attack
6. Cock sparrowhawk	very strong fear: *hewie* note and spasmodic fluttering of wings

The robin shows off its red breast in an aggressive posture, which is intended to scare off an intruder – in this case a stuffed robin!

below, for example, from willow warblers to stuffed predators and a cuckoo near their nest.

Clearly, this study indicates that a willow warbler can differentiate a cuckoo from a hawk; the former can be attacked, the latter is to be feared. The falcon was interesting because its general colouring and shape resembled the cuckoo (despite the hooked beak), so it is fairly certain that willow warblers have a concept of 'cuckoo' associated with a blue-grey head.

4. In autumn, some chiffchaffs (or willow warblers, for they are difficult to identify at that season) seem to resent the close proximity of any other small bird and will madly chase for metres another warbler or finch. Similarly, pied wagtails on migration, particularly on the seashore, will pursue other wagtails, pipits and even waders such as dunlins and turnstones. The reasons why these birds are so aggressive are not clear and would be worth discovering.

5. In defence of territory, we usually notice that the cock bird is being aggressive. What aggressive display do you see from hens? What forms of display do you see at the bird table as you work out a peck order (*see* Project 24), and are both sexes involved?

6. At a feeding station, observe the aggressive display of greenfinches. How often does display (raised wings and a lunge with open bill) become an aerial fight? Is such a fight only between males? Do both return to the food?

7. Carefully observe when aggressive display is linked with a call different from other calls and so is clearly a signal denoting aggression. The blackbird's repeated chink is an example.

Injury Feigning

Some birds are so demonstrative in defence of their young that they display madly before a predator to try and distract its attention.

An extreme form of the distraction display is injury feigning, for example when a duck mallard pretends to have a broken wing and flounders ahead of a fox until the beast has been lured to a safe distance from the ducklings. So few distraction displays have been carefully studied that there is wide scope for amateur research, especially among such ground-nesters as ducks, waders, nightjars, larks and pipits.

Data could be collected under these headings: (a) How far does the behaviour take place from the nest or chicks? (b) Which sex displays most and what does the other partner do meanwhile? (c) How successful is injury feigning in deceiving man or beast? (Even an authority on bird display, E.A. Armstrong, admits to being deceived once by a ringed plover); (d) Do other birds of the species join in, as happens in the communal display of pratincoles?

Pratincoles are gregarious birds, both during and outside the breeding season. A whole colony will fly up together on the approach of a predator, and will mob a crow or harrier. Injury feigning by several birds at once has been often recorded; sometimes the behaviour is so intense that the 'injured' bird appears to be dying.

Apart from records for a few other ground-nesting birds, such as divers, the nightjar and short-eared owl, there are few records of injury feigning or even distraction displays from birds which do not nest on or near the ground. Fluttering crippled-looking flight has been recorded from nesting willow warbler, blackcap and nuthatch. Nesting blue and great tits hiss and flick their wings. If you have put up several nest boxes in a wood a description and analysis of this behaviour would be very worthwhile.

Injury feigning is a desperate attempt by a bird, such as a lapwing, to prevent you, the predator birdwatcher, from finding its nest, or young, which are running free. It means you are close to one or the other and so are in danger of treading on eggs or chicks. Observe carefully and quickly, and leave the area to watch from a safe distance, so that you can be sure you do not distress the birds anymore and do not break the law (*see* Introduction to Chapter 2).

DISTRACTION-LURE DISPLAY

This display, which tries to distract a predator and lure it away from the nest, takes several forms and is best observed among the waders. In order, from passive to most active, you may observe:

1. The bird runs a few metres, then freezes.
2. A crouching run, with plumage sleeked, away from the intruder (the so-called 'small mammal run').
3. A crouching run, back humped, tail fanned and depressed, sometimes with quivering primaries (the 'rodent run').
4. The bird pretends to be injured; it creeps along, feathers ruffled, tail fanned and often tilted towards the predator ('injury feigning'); sometimes one wing (or even both) is dragged along, the wing-tip touching the ground (the 'broken wing' trick).

Plovers, in particular, use these displays. They are quite startling to observe.

A ringed plover giving the broken-wing display.

Roosting

Every evening, birds go to roost, usually in thick, safe cover. Some, such as gulls and waders, roost in vast numbers, which are exciting and comparatively easy to study.

Most of us do not watch our nestboxes carefully outside the breeding season. If we did we might be rewarded by seeing tits or wrens going to roost. Many have been found in one box!

Blackbirds and sometimes robins roost together in thick conifers but it is even more difficult to track down where single birds, like a song thrush, dunnock or chaffinch, roost. However, some species, like waders, wildfowl and gulls, roost in open places where it would be difficult for a predator to reach them. Other species, such as starlings and jackdaws are noticeable before they even get to roost, as they fly regularly on the same route to the roosting site.

The lines of research below could be applied to the study of many species that can be traced to roost:
1. Period of time covering arrivals and departures at the roost.
2. As in (1) but related to weather and season.
3. Numbers roosting.
4. Roosting sites.
5. Behaviour on arrival and departure.
6. Flight lines to and from roosts.
7. Origin of roosting birds.

Autumn and winter are the best seasons to watch all this, and it is not too difficult to find roosts of starlings, finches, jackdaws,

WRENS ROOSTING
9 in an old song thrush's nest
10 squeezed into a coconut shell
17 in an old nest in a stable
22 in a house martin's nest
46 in a nestbox
60–70 darting about a hen coop where they probably roosted

(Data from Armstrong 1955.)

swallows, martins, gulls, waders, blackbirds and redwings. One example will suffice to illustrate the potential interest in this project. One February, PJ Dare and I noted many redwings flying south of south-west over Exeter every evening. We plotted a line on a map, cycled to several more watching points and eventually discovered a roost of about 2,000 birds in firs and laurels 2.5 miles (4km) from where we first saw the birds. By early March, the roost numbered around 6,500, a spectacular sight, which amply repaid the cold watch and wait over several nights.

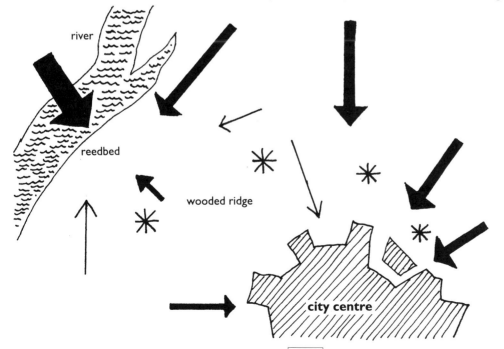

Tracking down starlings' roosts from observations at four points (indicated by stars on the diagram). The arrows show the directions in which starlings were seen flying from the observation positions.

river

reedbed

wooded ridge

city centre

6. THE NUMBER OF BIRDS

*The more we know how many birds breed and winter each year
in the British Isles, the better we shall be able
to look after our natural heritage.*

How many birds are there? This is one of those childish questions asked in the sincere hope of an easy, satisfying answer. Unhappily it falls into the 'How long is a piece of string?' category. It all depends.

The reply could be made in at least half a dozen different ways:

1. The number of different kinds of birds in the world.
2. The number of individuals of a species in the world.
3. The number of individuals of a species in a certain part of the world.
4. The number of birds of each kind in a given habitat.
5. The total number of all individuals of all kinds of birds in the world or a given part of it.
6. The number of different kinds of birds recorded by the observer.

Numbers of birds intrigue not only children but also birdwatchers, who cannot but be excited by a coastwise passage of thousands of seabirds, a roost of 100,000 starlings or even a single something if it happens to be the first to be seen. The careful scientific counting of bird numbers is a relatively modern pursuit, despite the lead given by that genius-naturalist Gilbert White in the late 18th century.

In a letter to the Hon. Daines Barrington, White anticipated by 150 years or more, the modern studies of animal population, census work and life-tables. Having made a count, such as the eight pairs of swifts counted by White, the observer should not leave it at that, but ought to learn more of the whys and where-

> ## GILBERT WHITE'S 39TH LETTER TO THE HON. DAINES BARRINGTON
>
> Among the many singularities attending those amusing birds, the swifts, I am now confirmed in the opinion that we have every year the same number of pairs invariably; at least the result of my enquiry has been exactly the same for a long time past. The swallows and martins are so numerous, and so widely distributed over the village, that it is hardly possible to recount them; while the swifts, though they do build in the church, yet so frequently haunt it, and play and rendezvous round it, are easily enumerated. The number that I constantly find are eight pairs; about half of which reside in the church, and the rest build in some of the lowest and meanest thatched cottages. Now as these eight pairs, allowance being made for accidents, breed yearly eight pairs more, what becomes annually of this increase; and what determines every spring which pairs shall visit us, and reoccupy their ancient haunts?... Whether the swallows and house martins return in the same exact number annually is not easy to say, for reason given above; but it is apparent, as I have remarked before in my Monographies, that the numbers returning bear no manner of proportion to the numbers retiring.

fores, as well as the how-manys. Whatever projects about numbers of birds the observer decides to follow, whether the simplest or the most taxing in time, energy and knowledge, he should never fail to ask questions as White did.

CENSUS AND COUNT

It is as well to define two words of importance connected with the science of bird numbers: census and count. A census usually refers to the counting of a breeding population, whereas the count is more often used to number the wintering flocks of gregarious species, especially gulls, waders and wildfowl. Counts provide a vast amount of information on the distribution and movements of the winter population, data that has proved invaluable in the selection of a network of wildfowl refuges. A census (the estimate of a particular population) can enable the scientist to work out annual fluctuations in population, discover the causes of any fluctuations and perhaps, if continued long enough, determine definite trends in numbers. Such information is invaluable in modern conservation work, whether it be to help declare a new nature reserve or a Site of Special Scientific Interest (SSSI); or to contest the building of a motorway.

Black-headed gulls feeding in late October over storm-driven seaweed at St Mary's lighthouse, Northumberland.

There have been in modern times three main approaches to the science of bird numbers:

1. Efforts have been made to work out the answer to the question, 'How many species?' But there is no accord because some disagree about the separate validity of species which are considered genuine by others. There are about 8,600. It is only recently that the water pipit and the rock pipit, the crossbill and the Scottish crossbill have been classified as separate species; many bird books still show the latter of each pair as a subspecies of the former.

2. Certain species have been censused in great detail. The four conditions under which the world population of any bird can be accurately established were suggested by Fisher (1954): (a) that they are social seabirds with a limited number of colonies, and a definite breeding season, so that expeditions can count the number of occupied nests at each colony; (b) that, if land birds, they are social birds with a restricted geographical distribution and a limited number of colonies; (c) that they are large and spectacular birds, easy to recognize, which are nearly extinct or which have a relatively small breeding area in which the territory or hunting ground of each individual pair can be discovered; (d) that they are species of birds restricted to small islands.

Fisher adds that at considerable expense and with well-coordinated manpower, many colonies of a social species could be counted over a wide area, so obviating problems (b) and (c); condition (a) having been satisfied it is known that the world gannet population is about 213,000 breeding pairs (Nelson, 1978). Under (b), careful studies of pink-footed geese have revealed only three breeding areas in the whole world: Iceland, Greenland and Spitzbergen. Up to 10,000 pairs nest in one colony at Thjorsarver in Iceland, 2,000 pairs elsewhere in Iceland, 1,000 in Greenland and maybe 4,000 pairs in Spitzbergen. All the last named birds and their young winter in the Netherlands; all the rest winter in Britain. Conditions (c) and (d) are more easily fulfilled, once the breeding area is known. For example, there are about 150 whooping cranes in North America, about twelve crested ibises in Japan and China, about 100 pairs of giant grebes, all on one lake in Guatemala, and fewer than twenty echo parakeets on Mauritius.

3. Despite the seemingly insurmountable problems, there have been a few attempts to number all the birds of all species in one country. In Finland (see special review, Nicholson, 1959), a scientist estimated just over 32 million breeding pairs for the recorded 130 species, with the willow warbler proving to be the commonest with 5,700,000 breeding pairs – a truly pioneering effort. Pioneering studies in Great Britain, organized by the BTO (see Projects 48, 49 and 63), have given us details of the numbers of breeding and wintering birds in Britain. The results are in *The Atlas of Breeding Birds* (1976), *The Atlas of Wintering Birds* (1986), *Population Trends in British Breeding Birds* (1990) and *Britain's Birds* (1991).

That is a long way from Gilbert White's humble count of the swifts in his village. The projects that follow start with ideas that are simple and personally satisfying, and end with more complex projects, which could lead to valuable scientific results.

Tick Lists

Even today, the age of conservation and bird protection, men are hunters, but instead of having a cabinet full of specimens at home, they now have tick lists.

Perhaps the first tick list any ornithologist makes is a life list, that is a list of all the species he has ever seen. Some subdivide the list if they are lucky enough to travel abroad, and keep the 'home country' list separately from the 'seen abroad' list. It is useful to record in a card index or master log-book or computer database details of first sightings.

The computer database is the most useful way of storing and retrieving information. Each system should record at least: date first seen; where seen; further remarks. Under the last heading could be added later sightings, or a note about a rare species being accepted by the Rarities Committee (*see* Chapter 1). Needless to say any 'first' should be recorded in detail in the observer's field notebook.

The life list is just an exciting summary of records, it is not a substitute for the notebook. It is a project that never ends, and how long the list is depends more on how far you are able to travel than on how much time is available.

My jogging along over forty years has enabled me to see just over 400 species, a low total compared with some of my more widely travelled friends, but nevertheless I am happy to see usually two 'new' species a year. This pales to insignificance when compared with the world life lists of Harvey Gilston of Switzerland and John Danzenbaker of the United States, both of whom have seen over 6,800 species around the world.

An obvious variation on this list is to put at the end of each year's field notebook a list of all the birds seen in that year. In Britain, 100 is a comfortable target for the regular watcher. To get to 150 means more miles and being out and about regularly; 200 is hard work. And as far as I know, very few have reached the magical 300 in a year within the United Kingdom, an achievement which may mean travelling over 50,000 miles, having time off work, and spending hundreds (even thousands) of pounds on transport!

Besides a life list, the watcher could keep a garden list, a parish list, an estate list or a county list.

VARIOUS TICK LISTS

- Life list of all species seen
- United Kingdom list
- Foreign list of all species seen outside the United Kingdom
- Total species seen in a year or each month
- List of species seen in your garden
- Parish list
- County list
- Holiday list

TIPS TO ACHIEVE 100 IN A DAY

Plan the day. Give careful consideration to:

- the time of year, to gain as many migrants and as much reasonable weather as possible; May is a popular month for an attempt;
- a range of habitats, so important for an expectation of a variety of species;
- a knowledge at first hand of areas to be hunted;
- a careful study of local bird reports to identify good places to visit which are not on your usual 'beat';
- the trip being a team effort, perhaps three or four of you – the more pairs of eyes the better.

You never know when they might be useful.

Anyone hoping to achieve the birdwatcher's equivalent of the four-minute mile – 100 species recorded in a day – must not rely on luck, but on good management.

'Tick-hunting' is quite a sport now in Britain and North America. National and local bird clubs organize sponsored day and year lists to raise funds for the organization and conservation projects. Even 150 species in a day have been seen within one county boundary (Norfolk). How well can you do?

It is to be hoped that a birdwatcher's interest in the number of birds will become more serious and scientific than simply chasing around after new ticks, although it would be a sad day if he stopped twitching altogether.

PROJECT 45

Counting Birds

' Counting, one way or another, is necessary if we are to give precision to any of the statements we make about the distribution of birds ...' (Yapp 1962).

In olden days, miners took a caged canary into the mine as a safeguard against an unseen danger: a dead canary meant dangerous gases and the miner had just enough time to get out before he too succumbed. Today, the world is the mine, wild birds the canary, and we are the miner. We must take care of that canary. This project, and the rest in this chapter, all demonstrate ways of counting birds so that we can scientifically assess their numbers from year to year, and from place to place. Such information is invaluable in conservation work; for example, in helping an organization to establish a new Site of Special Scientific Interest (SSSI) or manage properly an existing reserve.

Large flocks of waders, like these dunlin, are very hard to count.

It is not easy to count accurately the birds in a large flock. It takes practice. Large flocks may have to be estimated. Count ten birds and then estimate how many tens there are. Very large flocks can be estimated in hundreds. Practice will improve the accuracy of the count, but even experienced counters readily admit that they are often as much as 20 per cent out in their estimations. If time allows, of course, a flock should be counted accurately, or at least several estimations should be compared and an average accepted.

RULES FOR COUNTING

1. Count carefully.
2. Count again, as a check.
3. Record accurately.
4. Keep all your original notes.
5. If you write your notes up for publication, quote the original figures, or,
6. If you use percentages, give such information so that your crude figures can be calculated.
7. Your figures must not be wrapped in complicated mathematics; their meaning must be clear.

PERCENTAGE FREQUENCY

One of the quickest ways of comparing the occurrence of birds in different areas is using a counting method called 'percentage frequency'. For example, the species in several small woods or in each square kilometre in the observer's district can be compared. The areas must, of course, be comparable in size. As large a number of sample areas (or quadrats) as possible is observed and the species present in each of them are recorded. No notice need be taken of the number of individuals present. The number of plots containing a particular species is expressed as a percentage of the species. For example, in fourteen quadrats, chaffinches are in seven, wrens in twelve and house sparrows in two. The percentage frequency of each is thus 50, 86 and 14 respectively.

Instead of using sample plots as a base for observations, a time quadrat (a certain time unit such as a quarter of an hour) may be used. Each species recorded in a time-quadrat is recorded, and the number of time units containing a certain species is expressed as a percentage of the total number of time units.

A series of carefully recorded counts may be used to see whether two species are associated together more often than one would expect by chance. A simple correlation formula can be used:

$r = ad/bc$
r = the coefficient of association or correlation
a = total number of quadrats
b = number containing the first species
c = number containing the other
d = number containing both

The result can never be less than zero:
1 (unity) = what would be expected by chance;
less than 1 = the two birds occur less often than would be expected
more than 1 = they occur more often than would be expected

A particularly high or low value will indicate a strong association or the reverse, but why that is so is another problem which will need to be solved.

Counting Seabirds

The numbers of seabirds breeding on the coasts of Britain are of international importance. It is therefore vital to know the location and size of the colonies holding these birds.

An ever-growing band of bird-watchers spends hours (especially in or after autumn gales) watching seaward, eyes glued to high-powered binoculars or a telescope, counting seabirds on migration. Much has been learnt in recent years about the movements of Atlantic and North Sea seabirds thanks to these tough, dedicated stalwarts. If there is a headland near you, visit regularly, especially with an onshore wind. St Ives in Cornwall has become famous for its north-westerlies in autumn which drive close to the watching point on St Ives Island hundreds of Manx shearwaters, auks and gannets, and great rarities such as Wilson's petrel, long-tailed skua and Sabine's gull. Careful study of gulls at roosts, rubbish tips or feeding together at sewage out-falls has revealed some regular visitors which hitherto had been considered rarities, such as the Mediterranean and ring-billed gulls.

Exciting though some isolated visits may be, regular watching and counting are more important. Seabirds provide an effective way of monitoring the quality of the marine environment. They can be used as indicators of marine pollution (*see Project 53*) and changes in food availability. We were immediately aware of the horror of the former when we watched news-reels of the birds caught in the oil spills of the Gulf War in 1991; not so well known by the general public are the deaths of tens of thousands of seabird chicks in the Shetland Islands between 1988 and 1990. Kittiwake and arctic tern chicks starved to death because there were not enough sandeels to feed them although the possible rôle of over-fishing by man is unclear. Fortunately in 1991 these birds

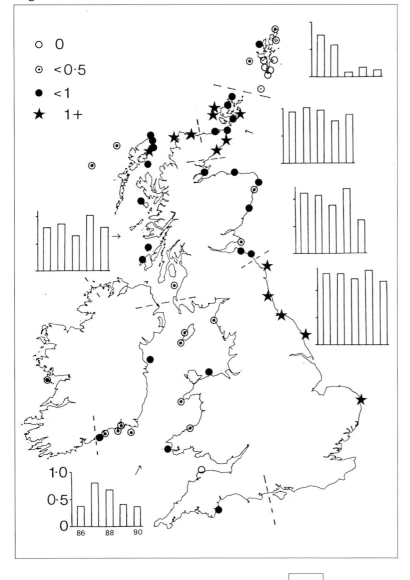

This map shows breeding productivity (number of chicks fledged per well-built nest) at kittiwake colonies, 1986–1990. The colony symbols indicate 1990 figures for individual colonies. The histograms indicate annual variation in average productivity for six subdivisions of the coastline (based on colonies studied in 1990). Reproduced from Walsh et al. (1991).

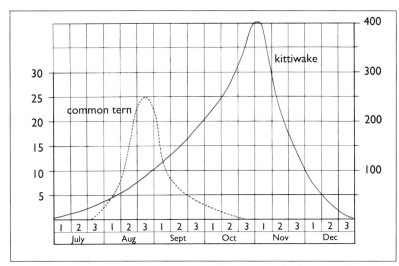

Above: records of a series of sea-watches from Point Lynas, Anglesey, made over several years. The vertical axes show the mean number of common terns and kittiwakes passing the point per hour for the four hours after dawn. Each month has been divided into thirds (1st–10th, 11th–20th and 21st–30th). The graphs show clear peaks of migration (data courtesy of PJ Dare).

Below: kittiwakes breeding on the limestone ledges of Bempton Cliffs, an east coast RSPB reserve.

had a much better breeding season.

Breeding seabirds' numbers are monitored in order to assess the population changes, productivity, survival and food supply at colonies. To this end, two internationally important studies are being organized by the Seabirds Team of the Joint Nature Conservation Committee in conjunction with the Royal Society for the Protection of Birds, the Shetland Oil Terminal Advisory Group at Aberdeen University, the Seabird Group and others. These studies are The Seabird Monitoring Programme (since 1989) and the Seabird Colony Register (since 1985). Despite the publication of the results of surveys done so far (it is very interesting to compare Cramp *et al.*, 1974, with Lloyd *et al.*, 1991) there are still gaps in coverage which need to be filled.

MONITORING SEABIRDS

To provide a comprehensive picture for Britain and Ireland there is still much useful work to be done. Contact the Seabirds Team (for address see page 125) for guidance.

1. There are particular gaps in the coverage of cliff-nesting species along the south coast of England and much of Ireland.

2. However, almost everywhere helpers are needed to follow population changes, at a particular colony or on a defined stretch of coastline by means of annual counts of some or all species. For most species this would involve a single count of apparently occupied nests each year, best timed between early to mid-June (guillemot and razorbill individuals are ideally counted five to ten times during the first twenty days of June to allow for day-to-day variations).

3. Information on breeding success is assessed at few colonies at present. The kittiwake is a good subject and a particular effort is being made to monitor that species. Best results come from regular (seven or ten day) checks, but a visit soon after egg laying (end of May) and another prior to fledging (mid-July) can produce useful data.

4. Knowledge of the distribution and numbers of nocturnal seabirds (for example Manx shearwater and storm petrel) is very incomplete.

5. Inland seabirds (for example common and black-headed gulls and common tern) have never been counted comprehensively.

The National Waterfowl Counts

All ducks, geese and swans are counted, and the coverage is now so good that trends in the European population of migratory wildfowl, especially ducks, are kept under annual review.

Anyone who wants to put counting birds to good use should endeavour to take part in one of the nationally administered regular surveys. The National Waterfowl Counts were instigated in 1947 and have been kept going by thousands of volunteers ever since. Their records are collated, analysed and published by scientists working at The Wildfowl and Wetlands Trust, Slimbridge (for address *see* page 125). Coverage throughout Great Britain and Northern Ireland is co-ordinated by voluntary regional organizers. If you would like to help, contact Slimbridge to find out who your local organizer is. Nearly 2,000 wetland sites are counted every winter at least once; ideally, each site should be counted once a month from September to March, on fixed dates. Some areas are difficult to visit regularly; others, such as large estuaries and bays, are hard to cover well without a team effort. Helpers are always welcome, even in what are generally thought of as well-watched counties. Each helper receives an annual report which summarizes the monthly count for every species, and gives a commentary on the numbers.

The monthly wildfowl counts and special surveys provide the basic data for conservation and management of wetland sites, and help provide valuable information to safeguard sites from development. If a site regularly has 1 per cent of the known population of a species or subspecies or holds regularly a total of 20,000 waterfowl it is a site of international importance. Over twenty sites in Britain regularly hold over 20,000 ducks, geese and swans, and waders as well.

DID YOU KNOW?

● The British wintering population of the dark-bellied brent goose (it breeds in arctic Siberia) has grown dramatically in line with a ten-fold increase in the world population. It has been discovered that breeding follows a three-year pattern: one good, one poor, and one which could be either. In 1989, only twenty-two juveniles (they have distinctive plumage) were identified in winter flocks, out of a grand total of 39,000 geese which were aged!

● A rapid increase in the number of shelducks breeding inland has taken place in the past twenty years. No one knows why.

● Gadwall are at least ten times more common now than in the 1960s.

● As the British ruddy duck population expands it may well compete with native wildfowl. If you record aggressive behaviour between a ruddy duck and another species send the details to The Wildfowl and Wetlands Trust (for address, see page 125), noting: other species, the initiator, the victor, and the immediate effects.

TOTAL NUMBERS OF WILDFOWL COUNTED IN GREAT BRITAIN IN EACH MONTH 1989–1990: A SELECTION FROM OVER 30 SPECIES RECORDED

Species	Sep	Oct	Nov	Dec	Jan	Feb	Mar
Mute swan	11,640	12,242	11,745	10,643	12,616	10,161	8,453
Canada goose	33,664	28,772	31,483	29,860	34,015	26,071	20,210
Shelduck	18,907	34,216	57,879	59,952	74,059	63,029	50,058
Mallard	156,013	160,613	157,440	169,865	181,062	109,464	61,710
Shoveler	7,132	8,157	6,278	5,755	5,829	4,929	4,900
Smew	0	1	3	40	57	53	38
No. of sites	1,331	1,404	1,433	1,415	1,707	1,461	1,450

Above: Brent geese are very sociable birds, forming huge winter flocks on estuaries.

Right: results of counting the number of gadwall present nationally in November and December. Despite a constant proportion of gravel-pit counts (bottom graph), the number of gadwall visiting gravel pits has increased at the expense of natural lakes.

SOME INTERNATIONALLY IMPORTANT WILDFOWL SITES IN GREAT BRITAIN

Loch Neagh/Beg	82,677
Wash	67,545
Ouse Washes	64,109
Ribble Estuary	57, 417
Loch of Strathbeg	40,922
Solway Estuary	37,673
Abberton Reservoir	33,986
Lindisfarne	30,569
Montrose Basin	30,270
North Norfolk Marshes	30,077
Mersey Estuary	29,422
Thames Estuary	29,363
Dee Estuary	26,272

Based on the average counts in the seasons from 1985–86 to 1988– 89 of wildfowl, grebes, cormorants and coots.

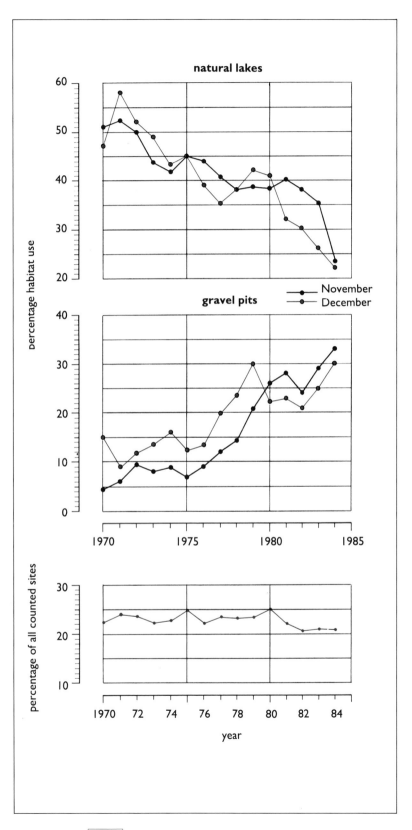

The Common Birds Census I

This is an annual census of breeding birds which provides information on which birds are found where in our countryside, and how their numbers are changing over the years.

Many garden birdwatchers today are aware that there are not as many song thrushes as there were a few years ago, and as many fiercely argue that there are far more magpies, and that they must be having a harmful effect on garden birds. Such observations are subjective: scientific evidence would be needed to prove the decline or increase. That evidence is at hand. One of the most important bird books ever written, *Population Trends in British Breeding Birds*, was published in 1990. It is compulsory reading for every birdwatcher and conservationist, and is based on observations of hundreds of amateur birdwatchers who have taken part in the Common Birds Census of the British Trust for Ornithology. Its findings confirm the increase of the magpie and the decline of the song thrush. *Population Trends* details the health of the populations of 160 of our breeding birds, particularly those nesting in farmland and deciduous woodland. New plots are now needed to reverse the current decline and to allow monitoring to continue strongly into the 1990s.

The CBC, as it is popularly known, was started in 1962. It relies entirely on about 300 volunteers each year who must complete ten to twelve full visits to the agreed site. A farm plot should have an area of about 60 hectares (150 acres), and a woodland plot should be about 10 hectares (25 acres).

The census depends on the observer using the mapping technique, refined by the BTO, and now much used throughout the world. On a large scale map, preferably 1:2,500 (about 25 inches to the mile) the observer writes a sign for each bird he sees or hears (*see* sample map opposite), in the correct place (the scale allows for the detailed marking of hedges, tracks and isolated trees so accurate plotting is possible). Each species is identified by a unique initial or pair of initials, for example B = blackbird, WW = willow warbler.

It is important to maintain CBC studies on farmland where farming practices, such as trimming or grubbing out hedges, affect bird populations.

Additional shorthand gives further information which will be of value in the final analysis (*see* panel).

Bird calls and songs will need to be well known; much of a visit will depend on you identifying birds in that way. Ideally, visits should be made in favourable weather when song is at its best; windy, damp days make birds depressed as well as birdwatchers. I have found that to complete a full series of ten to twelve maps in a season from late March to early July, over forty hours needs to be spent on each year's fieldwork. What happens to the maps is explained in the next project.

CBC FACTS

- Between 200 and 300 plots are covered each year by a band of volunteers.

- More than 40,000 territories are mapped each season.

- Since 1961, about 7,500 censuses have been made on 1,412 different plots.

- Computerized data on about 1.4 million birds' territories is stored by the BTO.

- All this data has been used in over 400 publications and several planning enquiries.

SYMBOLS USED ON COMMON BIRD CENSUS MAPS

B is for blackbird

Ⓑ is a singing male

B♀ is a hen giving an alarm

—2B♂— shows two fighting males

*B pinpoints a nest

B➤ movement shown by an arrow

Ⓑ---Ⓑ two rival males singing against each other

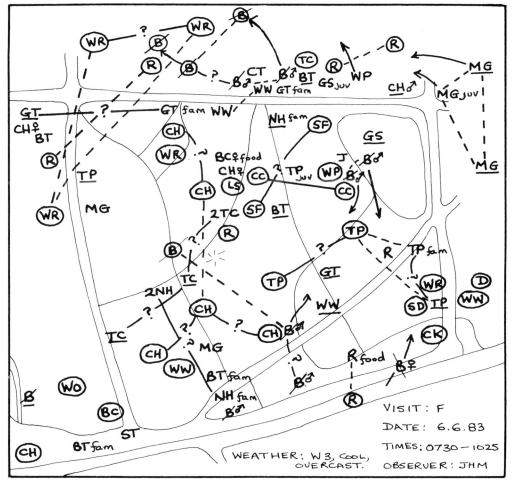

Part of a completed visit map for a woodland census. It was a productive visit and all parts of the map are crowded with registrations. The dotted lines will be particularly helpful in the later analysis of territories. Blackbird registrations have already been copied to the species map (see page 93) and cancelled with a light stroke of the pen.

VISIT: F
DATE: 6.6.83
TIMES: 0730 – 1025
WEATHER: W3, COOL, OVERCAST.
OBSERVER: JHM

The Common Birds Census II

The CBC provides a solid base for discovering, for example, whether a species is commoner or rarer this year, or whether habitat changes have affected a site's bird population.

The season's maps show every bird recorded. The observer then needs to produce a map for each species: so, each blackbird registration is plotted onto a new map, and so on. At the BTO, these species maps are analysed by specialist staff to discover how many territories of each species are present. A full account is then sent to the observer. These territory counts help to provide indices of population change for about seventy species. The index of a species is the measure of its change in abundance, relative to a chosen datum year in which the index value is set at 100. For most species, 1966 is the base year. The average index for the stock dove in 1978–87 was 629 which means the dove was about 6.3 times more common than it was in 1966. One can only compare like with like, in other words, one stock dove index with another. It is not a measure of abundance between species.

It is well known that farming methods are changing: field

THE WHITETHROAT

In 1969, birdwatchers everywhere found that whitethroats were suddenly scarce. The CBC was able to estimate that there was a 71 per cent decrease in the population in farmland and a 65 per cent decrease in woodland. This dramatic decrease was felt over much of Europe as far away as 15°E. It was attributed to disastrous mortality in the Sahel zone in Africa, on the southern edge of the Sahara where there was drought. CBC results have shown that the whitethroat has not yet recovered to pre-1969 numbers.

hedgerows and their big trees are disappearing still, even as other farmers are planting trees, or are using environmentally friendly

The edge of an oak wood in May, showing evidence of old coppicing. This is an ideal site in which to conduct a CBC.

PROJECT 49

farming methods. Census work is yielding results in the study of the ornithological potential of a wide variety of different habitats. Advice has been given in certain instances to help preserve native birds in the changing agricultural and forestry scene.

Our farms and forests and open spaces must be fit for British birds to live in. The data from birdwatchers who undertake CBC plots will help to make sure that the land is a fit environment for not only our rarities (which get plenty of publicity) but for our common birds, too. If you feel you cannot manage a CBC at present, try Projects 47, 62 or 63.

A male greenfinch, a common bird on the Common Birds Census in both farmland and woodland plots.

This is the blackbird species map from the same census as the example visit map on page 91. On transfer to the species map, the B for blackbird has been replaced in every case by the visit letter F, but the symbols indicating sex, song and movements have not been changed. The map has already been analysed, and six territories found on this portion of the plot, although two of these lie mostly beyond the northern boundary.

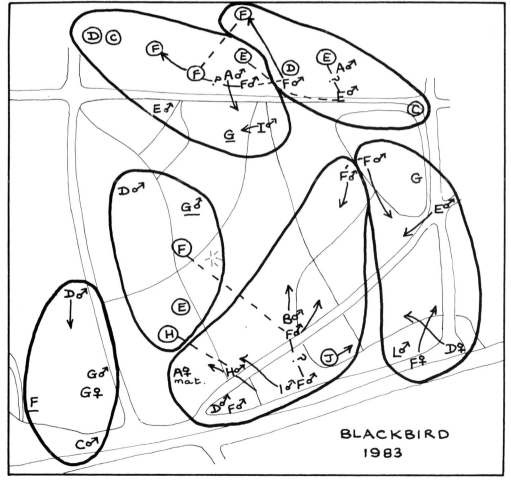

BLACKBIRD
1983

Ringing Birds I

The most effective way to mark a bird is to attach a small, numbered ring to its leg. This gives each bird a unique identity.

THE ORIGINS OF RINGING

Observing visible migration such as we have discussed in Project 38 can supply us with some excitement and answer some scientific questions. But until a bird can be individually identified, some things can never be known for sure: where exactly has the migrant come from? Where is it going? How fast will it travel? How long does a bird live? How faithful is an individual to a nest site?

Some of these questions were asked long ago. In the first bird book in English, *The Ornithology of Francis Willughby* (1678), it says,

'What becomes of swallows in winter time, whether they fly into other countries, or lie torpid in hollow trees, and the like places, on neither are natural historians agreed, nor indeed can we certainly determine. To us it seems more probable that they fly into hot countries, viz. Egypt Aethiopia etc.'

Nowadays we can determine where many species migrate, thanks to national bird-ringing schemes (or 'banding' as it is known in North America).

In about 1890, HCC Mortensen of Denmark was the first to use numbered metal rings. The first American numbered rings were used to mark herons in 1902; and in Britain, two schemes were started in 1909, one at the University of Aberdeen and one under the auspices of the *British Birds* magazine. (The former scheme amalgamated with the latter. It was taken over by the BTO over fifty years ago.) Now, there are ringing schemes throughout the world.

HOW TO BECOME INVOLVED IN RINGING

The first practical thing a birdwatcher might be expected to do in this project would be to report a ring number. If the bird is alive, trapped in a greenhouse, for example, handle it carefully, read

This male chaffinch has a BTO ring on one leg and a coloured ring on the other to help a scientist carry out a study of chaffinch territories.

SOME BRITISH RINGING STATISTICS

- There are just over 2,000 regular ringers.

- In recent years about 800,000 birds are ringed every year.

- About 14,000 ringed birds are recovered every year.

- Greenfinch, house sparrow, blue tit, blackbird and swallow have all passed the million mark.

- Since 1909, 20,826,038 birds have been ringed, of which 445,902 have been recovered.

(Mead & Clark, 1990)

TALE OF A ROCK PIPIT

I was watching rock pipits on a shore in South Devon when I found one with a light-blue ring over a dark-blue ring on the left leg, and a metal ring over an orange ring on the right leg. I wrote to the BTO and soon had a reply from the University of Gøteborg, Sweden!

The bird's story was as follows:

– Originally ringed as a chick 10th July 1985 on Nidingen Island, Sweden.

– Colour-ringed 26th April 1986 on the same island where it was breeding.

– Last seen there 17th July 1986.

-Seen at Wembury Point, Devon 5th March 1987.

This was the first proof that Scandinavian rock pipits were found in Devon, although it had been suspected, based on subtle plumage characteristics which differentiate it from our native rock pipits.

Many sedge warblers like this one are ringed all over the country each year. The unique number on its ring will enable its movements to be traced should it be caught elsewhere. Such movements would remain unknown were it not for ringing.

the number on the ring, *write it down*, and only then release the bird. Carefully remove the ring from a dead bird and tape that to your letter. All national schemes have their address on each ring, besides the bird's individual number. British rings are usually marked like this:

BRIT. MUSEUM
LONDON SW7
VJ 25615

or this:

BRITISH MUSEUM
LONDON SW7
RB 89740

Some rings are marked:

BTO TRING
ENGLAND
OH 8290

The museum address is a courtesy one now; all the records sent there are passed on to the BTO. Be sure to report the date the bird was found and exactly where it was found, what had happened to the bird, the species, your name and address, and most importantly, the ring number. Whatever the country of origin of the ring, the organizers of the scheme will send you the ringing details of the bird.

Besides the metal, numbered rings, ringers may sometimes use coloured plastic rings (some large ones on mute swans, for example, are big enough to be numbered), wing tags or even feather dyes so that birds may be instantly recognized in the field without needing to be retrapped. You should report these birds, too. Detailed studies of discrete populations are made possible by such colour rings; you have probably seen colour-ringed birds in television programmes about robins, bee-eaters, waders or scrub jays.

Each and every report of a ringed bird helps in a small way to complete our picture of that species' life history.

INFORM

Ringing Birds II

Trapping and ringing are skilled jobs, and in Great Britain, for example, no one can ring without first having successfully completed a training period.

Ringing birds is a skilled task. You need gentle hands, a sure touch, good co-ordination of hand and eye, patience and good control under stress (when being pecked hard by a greenfinch or stained by a blackberry-coloured dropping from a fidgety blackbird, for instance). The scheme is administered by the BTO which issues permits under licences covered by the Wildlife and Countryside Act, 1981, as amended by the Environmental Protection Act, 1990. A permit is issued for a year, with specific conditions attached.

The conditions are of roughly three kinds, restricting the ringer because of his inexperience to ring only adults not chicks in a nest, or to certain species, or to use only certain trapping methods. Firstly, anyone keen to be a ringer should contact a trainer, a highly qualified ringer who is on the BTO's list of trainers and who will introduce the would-be ringer to basic handling techniques and record keeping. Birds are caught in portable, small, automatic traps, large permanent cage traps such as the Heligoland trap, and mist nets. The last are much used because they are easily portable, can be set up quickly at suitable sites (such as a swallow roost) and are very effective because the net is almost invisible against a dark background. A ringer needs a special endorsement to use mist nets as well as traps. If you happen to come across a net set in a wood or in scrub on the coast do not attempt to release any birds – the ringer will be close at hand patrolling the site. Retire quietly, wait, then watch the ringer and learn exactly how it is done.

Several seasons and many birds later, a ringer may get a C permit. This entitles a person to ring without direct supervision, but under the guardianship of a trainer with whom the ringer must be regularly in contact.

Next, if a ringer wishes to progress to be fully qualified, it is necessary to attend a ringing course at a bird observatory. This will widen the ringer's experience of identification in the hand (very different from spotting a bird in a bush: colours, texture and size are amazingly different in the hand) and to improve handling, measuring and weighing skills. Then, with his trainer's blessing, the ringer may apply for an A permit.

This is not a project to treat lightly. It needs commitment. To achieve anything it will mean early mornings, careful planning, disappointment when the weather is bad, frustration when the garden trap is repeatedly blown

HOW QUICK ARE MIGRANTS?

Some recent speed records based on recoveries of ringed birds:

Sandwich tern	Lady's Island Lake, Eire	09.06.89
	to Durban Harbour, South Africa	12.12.89
	9,831km south of south-east. It had rounded the Cape of Good Hope!	
Curlew sandpiper	Fraena, Norway	04.09.88
	to Lough Beg, Eire	17.09.88
	1,538km south-west.	
Ring ouzel	Fair Isle, Shetland	22.10.87
	to Lannion, France	25.10.87
	1,206km south.	
Chiffchaff	Bardsey Island, Wales	10.05.89
	to Heligoland, Germany	18.05.89
	855km east.	
Goldcrest	Jurmo, Finland	06.10.88
	to Low Hauxley, Northumberland	22.10.88
	1,466km west of south-west	
Desert wheatear	Languard Point, Suffolk	23.10.87
	(where it was seen until the 25th)	
	to near Prawle, Devon 402 km WSW	26.10.87

(Had this rare bird not been ringed it would have been impossible to prove that the two records referred to the same individual.)

shut by the wind and catches no birds, persistence and patience. Then all is well when you catch a control (that is, a bird already ringed by someone else); or unexpectedly get a letter describing how one of your own ringed birds has been recovered, such as an immature blackcap I caught, ringed on 20th September 1986 which was found freshly dead, 28th September 1987 at Adiyaman, Turkey. This was the first British recovery in Turkey. Usually western European blackcaps migrate south-west towards north and west Africa; from about 15°E blackcaps migrate south-east. It is presumed that the one I had caught migrated on prevailing winds, or had reversed migration to Devon and had then reorientated to get on the right track for a member of the eastern population.

EXAMPLE OF A RINGING STUDY

There have been many in-depth studies of different species or groups of birds that have relied on ringing for their success. One on-going project is being run by Peter Rock on the roof-nesting gulls of central Bristol. He fits a single, very large (3.5cm/1.5in tall) plastic colour ring to the right leg of the gull chicks. A standard BTO ring is fitted to the left leg. Each colour ring is engraved to show a pair of letters and a different colour is used every year. In this way he is able to keep track of individual birds.

He has found that the herring gulls ringed in Bristol tend to remain in the South West and south Wales after fledging, and many stay in and around Bristol. The lesser black-backed gulls on

WHERE DO SWALLOWS GO IN WINTER?

Some recent recoveries:

Ringing site	Date ringed	Recovered	Date recovered
Happisburgh, Norfolk	28.09.85	Kapanga, Zaire	c. 15.10.86
Shrewsbury	10.08.87	Busia district, Kenya	13.01.88
Ballycotton, Cork	16.08.88	Windhoek, Namibia	29.12.88
Barnsley, Yorkshire	05.09.79	Orange Free State	30.01.87
Ipswich, Suffolk	22.09.85	Transvaal, South Africa	13.02.87

the other hand, move considerable distances. Peter's information shows that they travel as far as Spain, Portugal and North Africa. The furthest recovery though is from Nouakchott in Mauretania, around 4,000km (2,500 miles) from its place of birth.

The big gulls can live up to thirty years in the wild and Peter's long term aim is to piece together some of the details in the lives of the Bristol herring and lesser black-backed gulls. Some of them already have long life histories. He will be very pleased to send you details of any sightings you may make of the birds he has ringed if you write to him at 32 Kersteman Road, Redland, Bristol BS6 7BX.

This young herring gull (orange DP) was colour ringed in 1991 as part of Peter Rock's study on the roof-nesting gulls of central Bristol.

7. A VARIETY OF IDEAS

Like all good hobbies, birdwatching allows the participants to develop specialist skills: here one can be author, doctor, photographer, researcher and traveller.

Most birdwatchers have a favourite bird, or family of birds. For some it may be a spectacular species, for example, Leslie Brown (1955) wrote that 'Verreaux's eagle has one supreme quality, grace of flight; there is no more graceful flier in the world'.

The magnificent Verreaux's eagle.

In the 1940s, John Buxton was a prisoner of war in Bavaria. He determined to pass the time fruitfully studying a particular bird: 'I chose the redstart because of its grace and beauty, and for the sweet, gentle charm of its song' (Buxton 1950). Others single out what are apparently less attractive birds and are happy to spend many years watching them and trying to solve some riddles of their lives. One such writer was D Summers-Smith (1963), who declared that 'after twelve years of

watching, reading and thinking about sparrows I know there is much to be learned about them'. Most of us do not get further than thinking a house sparrow is just a tick on the list, but Summers-Smith found that with his chosen bird he was able to make observations 'at home and abroad and even in the most unlikely birdwatching localities as railway stations, the inside of factory buildings and from a dentist's chair!' I must admit that the only bird I have seen inside Tesco's is a house sparrow!

The dedication of these birdwatchers is an example to us all. Some others are mentioned in Project 54. Birdwatchers are sometimes dispirited when bad weather spoils a day out, or even when what other people call fine weather means that there is no visible migration to make an exciting day. The writers of

monographs such as *The Redstart* and *The House Sparrow* remind us that there is more to birdwatching than tick lists and spotting rarities. The excitement of the chase which ends with viewing a rarity is matched by the excitement of solving a bit of the puzzle of the life of a bird.

The robin, England's national bird and the subject of David Lack's famous monograph.

With some thoughtful planning of time and effort, birdwatching can become an absorbing hobby all the year round both indoors and outside.

The previous chapters have laid a heavy emphasis on fieldwork, and on looking for birds. Many of the ideas that follow will allow you to let the birds come to you as you watch from a hide, or a secluded corner in a reserve, or as you play armchair-detective with a bird book.

THE HOUSE SPARROW

' ... this well known and everywhere obvious bird ... '
Willughby & Ray (1678).

'Far too well known to need any description of its appearance or habits.'
Alfred Newton (d. 1907) founder of the British Ornithologists' Union and Professor of Zoology at Cambridge.

Chaucer (14th century) and Shakespeare (17th century) called the house sparrow 'lecherous'.

It still has rather derogatory or jocular nicknames, 'sprog' or 'spuggy'. But it usually keeps faithful mated pairs. It is found naturally across Europe and Asia; and has been introduced to the United States (from whence it spread to Canada and Mexico), South America, South Africa, Australia and New Zealand. It is an extremely sedentary bird, spending most of its life within 100m (110 yds) of its nest site.

It has become one of the most successful birds on Earth in its relationship with man.

DRAB BIRDS – FASCINATING LIVES

Corn bunting This bird has a strange song (with recognizable dialects) and a polygamous lifestyle.
Marsh tit/willow tit These two birds were not identified as separate species in the United Kingdom until 1897 and their distribution was not worked out until the 1930s. Can you find them both?
Grasshopper warbler It has a weird, reeling song which is sung with a ventriloquial effect, and so it is often heard but rarely seen.
Pipits These are 'little brown jobs' whose song-flights are well-worth studying.
Sand martins These are dull brown but live busy, colonial lives.
Spotted flycatcher This bird has drab colours, but is wonderfully active.

Hides

Hides can be useful for watching birds very closely without disturbing them. Hides are basically either permanent or portable.

Whichever species the observer turns to especially, it is at times when he is close to his quarry that he is particularly pleased. If this happens by chance it is exciting enough, but if one can by design get close views of a rare bird, a large flock of feeding wildfowl, or even a common bird at its nest, then this is ornithological heaven, such as it was for me when I watched my first black-winged stilts from a permanent hide at Albufera National Nature Reserve, Mallorca.

Anyone who has watched the finches and tits on the bird-table, from the hideaway of the living-room, knows that birds which would not come near if the observer was out in the garden can be closely watched. Provided the observer keeps still and makes no sudden movements or noise, some birds can be watched at the range of a foot or so on a table fixed to a window sill.

This principle of 'hide and let the birds come to you' holds good in the wild, as well as in your garden. Birds are very tolerant of material shapes close at hand but will scare quickly if a man approaches. A watcher from a car can drive slowly within very close range of a bird by a roadside, even wary birds such as redshanks, curlews and ducks, whereas a walker in the open would probably get no nearer than 20m (22 yds) or so. But a travelling car-hide clearly cannot go everywhere!

It is usually more convenient to build one, commanding a good view of a lake frequented by wildfowl, a wader feeding ground, a roost or a nest. There is often no need to use special materials; a satisfactory screen can be made from nearby natural materials, such as bracken, branches or reeds. The best one I remember making was of *Phragmites* reeds, on the edge of a reedbed, overlooking a mudflat on which godwits commonly fed. Reed stems laced horizontally among growing stems, a bit of judicious pruning, and the hide successfully and cheaply served its purpose. Sometimes a screen can be made by using only sacking on a frame of poles, which can then be camouflaged with sprigs of bracken, heather or whatever is handy. Such a frame

could be prefabricated, easily folded up or assembled, and used again and again.

A camper's toilet tent, with a viewing slit cut at a comfortable height compared with the observer's position on a folding stool, makes an excellent hide, especially when disguised with twigs or bracken. If you cannot trust your DIY skill, portable hides are regularly advertised for sale in birdwatching magazines.

With the permission of a landowner, a much more permanent

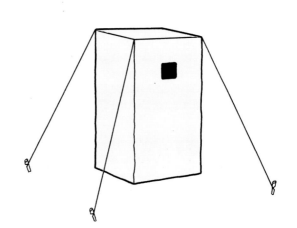

A simple hide made from a camper's toilet tent. It is essentially four poles, with a single piece of canvas over the top, tied down with guys at each corner and pegs around the bottom of the canvas. A viewing slit is cut to be at head height when the observer is inside sitting on a stool.

and elaborate hide of timber can be built. Such a hide may be invaluable in enabling a watcher to study ducks and geese undisturbed, as can be done at the Wildfowl Trust, Slimbridge by the River Severn, or the ospreys at the RSPB reserve at Loch Garten, Invernesshire. A permanent hide at a nature reserve enables several watchers to sit comfortably together. Perhaps the most spectacular hides have been those made from skins to look like a cow or a sheep, and the 18m (60ft) pylon hide made

A typical permanent hide. This one overlooks a good wintering ground for waders and wildfowl and is maintained by a local RSPB group.

in order to photograph a falcon's nest.

THE LAW

It is tempting to think that a hide will do no harm and will give the watcher the opportunity of hours of pleasure. The Wildlife and Countryside Acts, however, state that disturbance of nesting birds is an offence, and so no hide should be erected unless the bird's habits are known and one can be sure that they will not desert the nest. Some shy species may be watched from a hide only

If birdwatching in Majorca, one of the specialities that can be seen from the hides at Albufera is the black-winged stilt.

after it has been erected some distance away and slowly moved closer, over a period of several days.

Birds which are specially protected under the Acts may not be disturbed; any study at the nests of these species (*see* Chapter Two) can be carried out only after the receipt of a licence from the Nature Conservancy.

Although birds cannot count accurately, they do have some sense of number, and so two golden rules must be observed by watchers studying birds at a nest:

1. The nesting bird is aware of the arrival of 'man' at the hide, so it is disturbed and flies off. It may not return quickly, so jeopardizing the chances of survival of the young or eggs, unless 'man' is seen to leave the hide quickly. So, if two people arrive and one leaves immediately (leaving the watcher in the hide) all will be well because the waiting bird thinks all is clear.

2. If the watcher later explodes from the hide without warning, this could scare the nesting bird for good. So he must wait for a prearranged time to be relieved, or must signal a colleague, by waving a handkerchief out of the back of the hide, for instance. The assistant's arrival from a distance will disturb the brooding bird, naturally; the watcher can then be rescued, from cold, cramp, mosquitoes or even boredom (some birds may feed their nestlings only once every hour or so, thus creating only a few seconds of interest at the nest), and the bird will return when both people are away at a safe distance.

PROJECT 53

Sick and Injured Birds

Many birdwatchers find sick or injured birds and naturally want to look after them. This is difficult and often means that expert attention is needed, but bird hospitals are few and far between.

We can treat a bird for exhaustion and hypothermia due to being overcome by bad weather; and shock as a consequence of flying into a window. Keep the bird quiet and warm in a dark, lidded box for an hour or so, or perhaps overnight, to allow it to recuperate.

For a 'hospital' I have successfully used a wooden-frame cage with a wire-mesh front (1.3–2cm (0.5in or 0.75in) welded mesh is best) and hardwood sides, floor and roof. Most caged birds when scared try to fly up; if the box has a roof they will not do this. Line the floor with newspaper; renew it daily. Food and water pots should be fixed to prevent them being tipped over. To keep the bird really quiet, cover the cage with a cloth, as one does to quieten a canary.

Some birds, for example the crow family, are not too difficult to look after. But on no account should a bird be kept for longer than necessary, to a point when it seems tame and is dependent on you for food. Other species will be very taxing on time, patience, energy, ingenuity and money. During the course of running a bird hospital at school, we have looked after and released house

HOSPITAL FOOD

It *must* be carefully chosen:

- Wild-bird seed for finches, buntings, sparrows, doves.
- Soft-bill food (by mail order or from pet shops) for robins, thrushes, blackbirds, warblers.
- Mealworms for the 'soft-bill' species.
- Raw meat (with roughage such as fur, feathers or hair) for owls, birds of prey, crows and gulls.
- If in doubt, check the species' known diet in a good book.

sparrows, starlings, feral pigeons, herring gulls, black-headed gulls, oystercatchers, mallard, carrion crows, water rail (picked up in the gutter after a storm) wheatear, chaffinch and greenfinch.

This badly oiled guillemot at Ken Partridge's oiled seabird hospital has received first aid and is now ready to be washed.

PROJECT 53

This herring gull had a damaged wing. It was rescued and looked after by volunteer pupils at a school's bird hospital.

FIRST AID FOR AUKS

A. Preliminary tasks
1. Wipe off fresh oil with a cloth.
2. Clean the bill externally and internally to prevent more oil being swallowed.
3. Check for injuries. If present, contact the RSPCA.

B. Hypothermia
The bird must be warmed up.

C. Ingested oil
Oil which has been swallowed must be cleared out of the bird's system as quickly as possible before it is given food.

D. Feeding
An oiled auk may readily eat three or four sprats, or may be emaciated and need medical care and force-feeding.

Full details may be had from an RSPCA leaflet (for address see page 125).

We had disappointments, but the successes made up for that.

You should not take home 'orphan' fledglings. Newly fledged birds often become grounded. Put them in a bush near to where you find them; the adults will return and carry on feeding them.

Birds of prey are beautiful birds at the top of the food chain (*see* Project 34). They are particularly prone to poisoning, or injury by shooting by ignorant sportsmen and gamekeepers. Any effort to save such birds deserves success. However, they are specially protected by law, which means that even a vet cannot care for one for more than six weeks without a licence. Leonard Hurrell, who has for many years cared for injured falcons, hawks and owls, advises that you can be most helpful by taking your bird to a specialist (the RSPCA or a vet) who will then pass it on to the best local help available.

Anyone near the coast will sooner or later find an oiled seabird. Ninety-five per cent of these are guillemots and razorbills. The quicker a seabird can be cleaned and rehabilitated, the better. To minimize taming, try to leave it alone as much as possible. Do not pet it. Cleaning and caring for oiled birds costs time, money and patience. Using the following notes and those in the panel, think carefully before becoming involved.

Ken Partridge has considerable experience running an oiled seabird hospital, in conjunction with the RSPCA and the Southwest Oiled Seabird Study group. His following advice must be carefully considered.

Only after a bird is back to a healthy weight, and is fit enough, should the cleaning process commence. Full treatment, which takes three to four weeks, consists of a first wash in a 1 per cent solution of biodegradable washing-up liquid to remove the oil; a period of rehabilitation to ensure that the bird's feathers are waterproof; a second wash to remove dirt just before release; a final rinse to show that the feathers reject water all over the head, neck and body; two or three days in a water tank to ensure complete buoyancy and dry plumage; and finally, ringing and release, preferably at an auk colony. If you do want to help or to be helped, contact an RSPCA Oiled Seabird Unit (*see* page 125 for address).

Armchair Birdwatching

This project is for those frustrated birdwatchers who cannot get out watching on their day off because of ill health or bad weather.

Bird books are, with a few exceptions, expensive. The student of world birds can, however, at comparatively little cost (per purchase), build up a fine collection of illustrations of birds of the world by collecting foreign postage stamps. Single stamps or small sets may cost only a few pence and now that so many philatelists follow the thematic collection method, national post offices are only too willing to provide extra revenue for themselves by publishing new sets for collectors.

Once, when regretting that I could not afford to buy a new book about birds of the world costing several pounds, I turned out a cupboard and found my schoolboy stamp album, long forgotten but containing pictures of lyrebird and kookaburra from Australia, pied fantail and parson bird from New Zealand and a black-casqued hornbill from Liberia. Since then, the collection has grown to over 1,000 from 120 countries and territories, illustrating nearly 600 species. Mounted carefully in a looseleaf album, with a special note (common English name, scientific name, world distribution) beneath each stamp, the result is a self-made 'Birds of the World' volume.

Many of the stamps are beautiful examples of fine engravings or paintings and superb printing, and are the work of famous bird artists such as David Reid-Henry (Botswana), Don Ekleberry (British Honduras) and JJ Audubon (the United States and elsewhere). Some countries in recent years have produced sets 'advertising' conservation. The issue of such stamps heightens our awareness of the great need for conservation in every continent, and they help to educate the people who live in the land. Some good examples have come from Mauritius, the Seychelles, St Vincent and St Lucia, and all of them have featured very rare, endangered species.

If a birdwatcher maintains his own reference set of feathers, they can be useful in adding to his knowledge of the birds in a certain area. I have, for example, recorded tawny owl in a bird census wood on the strength of a fresh secondary feather, identified skylark as the prey of a merlin at a plucking post; and traced ptarmigan and golden plover in the Scottish highlands. The feathers come from road casualties, raptor plucking posts, gamekeepers, wildfowl collections, roosts and chance discoveries. Loose feathers can be mounted and labelled in a scrapbook. Wings from a dead bird can be opened and weighted each end; they will set after a week or so and will display all their colours and patterns. If treated with an insect-repellent powder they will last for years.

A fascinating piece of indoor research can be done by anyone who can read, copy and analyse the old game-books of a large keepered estate, or old parish and churchwarden records. A good gamekeeper kept a meticulous account of all gamebirds shot on the estate, especially partridges, pheasants and wildfowl.

READING PROJECTS

As soon as possible, familiarize yourself with the order in which bird families are scientifically arranged, that is, their classification. In the animal kingdom, birds are in the class known as *aves* which is divided into 28 *orders*, which in turn are divided into *families*, *genera* and *species*. All good field guides begin with a classification of our European birds from divers to passerines. Then, learn their Latin scientific names. Finally, start reading the splendid monographs (each book is devoted to the life of a species or family) now available, for example, on the barn owl, hen harrier, kestrel, robin, blackbird, wren, greenshank, swift and many more. Start with the very good series published by Shire Publications. Search your library and second-hand bookshops!

Details of bird life, numbers in particular, are very thin for years past and these books provide an almost unique, detailed look at birds in the 19th century. Little has been published of what may be found in these gamebooks. My own researches into game books for 1832 to 1906 of the Saltram Estate, Devon (*see* beginning of Chapter 1) were most illuminating and perhaps the most interesting indoor bird watching I have ever done.

A Birdwatcher's Year

Although the previous project illustrated the comforts of armchair birdwatching, a really committed birdwatcher will be out in the field every month of the year.

This book has suggested many things to do at different times of the year, but has tended to offer seasonal projects. This could give the impression that after the breeding season, birdwatching stops and does not start again until the wildfowl counts! The birdwatcher's fear, 'If I go out I won't see anything. If I don't go out I'm sure to regret it!', is sure to be backed up with recollections of experiences such as this one: I arrived by the shore in a gale and met a birdwatcher who said, 'Come to see the little auk? It was here ten minutes ago. It flew out to sea.' It is easy to give up then; the mystery of a 'bogey bird' grows (I still have yet to see a live Little Auk); and then some may believe that playing squash is a more certainly pleasurable pastime. But not the dedicated birdwatcher.

In Britain, there are birds to watch every month. Careful noting of each species each day in the same area can result in analyses of considerable interest.

One possible analysis is the song cycle. This is compiled by noting the days you hear the song of a particular species. The records are transferred to a bar diagram, blacking in each month the bird sings, like the one for the blackbird shown below.

Another analysis is to construct a pie chart representing for each species the percentage of all species that the chosen bird makes up, based on the number of contacts made over the year (*see* Projects 48 and 49 for detailed help in censusing). Lastly, a multiple bar chart can be used to compare the times of year several species are seen in your area based on contacts made as you watch each month. Watching throughout the year will enable you to build up a picture of a bird's annual cycle of behaviour in your part of the country.

The song period of the blackbird. The above trace (A) is the more usual duration; B is less likely.

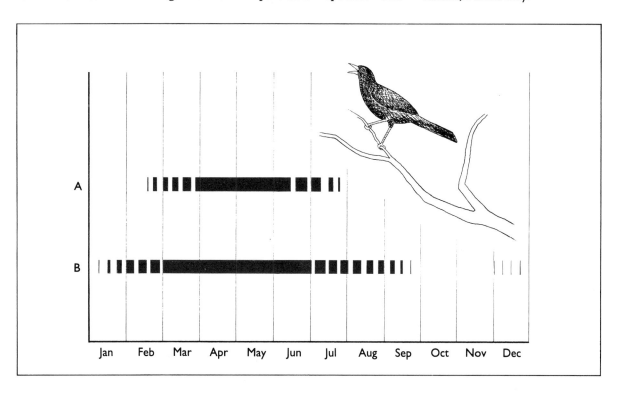

Photographing Birds

Photographs successfully satisfy man's desire for collecting birds. The hunt is often challenging after much planning, and the trophies (the photographs) are much more acceptable than a stuffed bird.

No other project apart from tape-recording depends so much on good equipment. Family pictures may look agreeable taken with a cheap instamatic camera, but these subjects are large; birds are small. It may be easy to photograph well a mute swan or a herring gull, but to get good slides or prints of small birds, special equipment is necessary. The photographer's binocular vision, which enables him to see in 3-D, deceives him into thinking the bird fills the picture. The camera tells no such lie.

Traditionally, birds have been photographed at the nest, and this form of portraiture still produces superb results. But because of the pressure on many rare birds it is unlawful to disturb willfully any birds included in Schedule 1 of the Wildlife and Countryside Acts. Thus photographers cannot lawfully visit a nest with eggs or young without a permit from the National Environmental Research Council (for address *see* page 125).

With the advantages given by the very portable 35mm camera, there is every opportunity to photograph birds in flight, bird behaviour and birds in their natural habitat. A tripod will ensure a steady platform for your camera; a hide will get you close to the birds but, increasingly, birdwatchers are finding that being as mobile as possible and stalking the quarry brings excellent results. Whether you work from a hide or stalk your birds, you will need to get closer than 10m (11 yds) even with a telephoto lens to get a good picture.

In the study of plants and insects, many beautiful photographs have been taken from very short range (a few centimetres). The resulting pictures are artistically delightful. Macrophotography, as this is called (good cameras have a macro-focusing stop), has been little practised on bird subjects since it is not easy to get close enough. But if an occasion arises, with a bird in the hand, for example, a picture of head or wing or bill could be very worth while. There can be few patterns to match that of the mantle feathers of a cock pheasant, the head of a teal or the wing of a barn owl.

To judge the worth of one's own pictures, one should look regularly at photographs in such magazines as *British Birds, Bird Watching* and *BBC Wildlife*. Self-criticism is vital. Study carefully books such as *A Field Guide to Photographing Birds* (Hill & Langsbury, 1988). Think about composition, colour, shadows, depth of field, range. And remember that many photographers come to accept that their most important piece of equipment is the bin!

Opposite: a grey heron. A good bird photograph is not always a close-up, but may reveal the bird in its habitat.

CAMERA TIPS I

Which camera?
You need a good single-lens reflex with interchangeable lenses. A basic camera usually has a 50mm lens or a zoom from 28m (wide angle) to 80mm (portrait telephoto), but a telephoto lens of at least 200mm focal length is needed for reasonable (or better) bird photographs; the camera should have a variety of shutter speeds up to 1/1000 of a second. Look carefully at the product reports in photography magazines and 'shop around', handling cameras before you buy. You will find prices range from £100 to well over £1,000.

Now birdwatchers are experimenting with video camcorders, using the 8x zoom plus a 1.5x telephoto converter. The results on the screen are exciting.

CAMERA TIPS II

Which film?
Single-lens reflex cameras take 35mm film. Most people today use colour film, although if you want to sell your pictures or show them at camera club exhibitions, black and white is still acceptable. Are you going to use print or slide film? The former gives excellent pictures for an album; the latter is essential if you intend to give lectures or have the picture published. It is best to buy a standard brand name. If you use slow film, rated at 25 or 64 ASA, you will get high-quality prints or slides; 100 or 200 ASA will give you more flexibility with the use of shutter speed and apertures, but will give you a more grainy picture.

PROJECT 56

Birdwatching Abroad

Once the birds of your own country become familiar and birdwatching has hooked you, birdwatching abroad will give your hobby a whole new dimension.

Whether you are going on a family package holiday, or deliberately on a camping birdwatching week, it is advisable to spend some time (and money) on research and planning so that whatever time you have at the resort for birdwatching is used to the best advantage.

Any birdwatchers in northern Europe who are familiar with a well-known field guide will sooner or later realize that their own personal life lists are not going to improve much unless a trip overseas is made. Budget and family commitments may dictate exactly where, but if you are relatively free of restraints and are planning the trip yourself, do take advice from, and book with, a reputable ABTA travel agent. Then your travel arrangements will be as trouble-free as possible.

Be sure to consult your GP about any inoculations; always take out travel insurance; and take a first-aid kit containing a good sun barrier cream, insect repellent, paracetamol tablets, water purifying tablets and a sun hat. If you are not relying on others to plan the business end of the holiday, do not forget to organize your travellers' cheques, passport, cash (with a money belt) and documents such as invoices to cover equipment that you are carrying so that you will not be charged customs dues. Be sure to have a new notebook and maybe a sketchbook and coloured pencils.

Before you go get to know your field guide well. Carefully check the species you are likely to see so that you are not completely at a loss when a new bird crosses your path. If possible, listen in advance to a good collection of bird recordings, especially those which cover woodland or scrub-loving species, which you are more likely to hear first than see.

Tips from friends who have already been to your chosen area are a great help. After personal help come maps, travel books and specialist publications.

If you intend travelling around at all, published maps of the area are an essential part of your kit. Not only will they guide you from place to place, but a careful study of them in advance will enable you to plan excursions to a variety of habitats: a wooded valley and up in the hills; a lake and a river system; rocky coastline or sandy shore and lagoons, and so on. Get to know an area well rather than dash around all over the place. Western Europe is well covered; Michelin maps are particularly good. If you can, shop around large bookshops, travel agents, AA and RAC offices to see what is available.

Your research should finally include a study of guidebooks. There are two kinds: those for holiday makers in general, and those specially published for birdwatchers. The former give detailed information, advice, illustrations and maps, country by country. Have a careful look at *Baedecker's (AA) Travel Guides, Michelin Tourist Guides* and Fodors guides. Further advice can be obtained from the national tourist offices of many countries; if you are going to the United States, Australia or Canada, splendid material can be obtained from each individual

Watching cattle egrets in Kenya! And look for weaverbirds and bee-eaters too.

PROJECT 57

Top left: *here in the Zagora Valley, Morocco, a birdwatcher might find white-crowned black wheatear, house bunting and long-legged buzzard.*
Bottom left: *Specialities in Switzerland, like the alpine*

chough, are easy to find at high altitudes. Not so easy lower down are citril finch and black woodpecker.
Right: *Birdwatching in the Rocky Mountains of Canada for Stellar's jay, North American wood warblers and bald eagle.*

state. The other books are publications specially designed to help birdwatchers abroad. From a library or a shop get *Where to Watch Birds in Britain and Europe* by John Gooders or *A Guide to Birdwatching in Europe* by J Ferguson-Lees *et al.*, and send away to get the small book covering your chosen country from one or more of the series published by Ornitholidays, Foreign Bird Reports and Information Service, and S Gauntlett. The

last named just provides checklists with a grid to enable you to tick species day by day, which is an ideal way to keep your holiday list going (*see* page 125 for the addresses of these sources).

Finally, if you have not already decided, where can you go? To Holland's coast for waders and seabirds and migrant rarities; to central or Atlantic coast France; the Alps for alpine accentor and citril finch (found only here and the mountains of

south-west Europe); the Mediterranean region for a completely new bird-world of bee-eaters, hoopoes and vultures; Morroco for a touch of Africa; or Israel for amazing migration watching. Maybe you have the chance to go further afield: to the United States or Canada, or the Gambia in West Africa? These visits will bring you in contact with birds of another continent, which are utterly different from our Western Palaearctic avifauna.

8. CONSERVATION

'The fact is that no species has ever had such wholesale control of everything on earth, living or dead, as we now have. That lays upon us, whether we like it or not, an awesome responsibility. In our hands lies not only our own future, but that of all other living creatures with whom we share the earth.'

(Sir David Attenborough, 1979, Life on Earth)

In the early days of national parks people needed to be persuaded to visit them. Now, managing traffic and walkers are major problems. Thanks to guidebooks, lectures, guided walks and television series on natural history there are so many visitors it is necessary to control where they walk and park their cars. In more recent years, mountain bikes have presented a problem.

The protection of a species depends on the survival of its habitat; and looking after that is conservation. In 1970, Alvin Toffler wrote in his influential book, *Future Shock*, that 'Education must shift into the future tense'. It certainly has. Books, television programmes, societies, retailers such as Body Shop and pressure groups have certainly been educating us about the future with the result that there have never been so many 'green' people.

We still need to hear Alvin Toffler's cry. We need the passion and commitment of Greenpeace, Friends of the Earth and individual conservationists who are good communicators to keep our minds on the future. Institutes of Education are helping too: a popular study course at The Open University is 'The Changing Countryside' for those who are professionally involved in the countryside; and other colleges and universities provide diploma and degree courses in countryside management. Being green is big business in politics, too. Indeed, if conservationists cannot forge an effective, personal, sympathetic relationship with politicians they might as well pack up. Government often has the

---

COMMUNITY FORESTS

The new community forest programmes in the United Kingdom are signs of the looking to the future. Community forests are multi-purpose: farmland, public open spaces and leisure facilities set in a well-wooded landscape. Each will cover between forty and eighty square miles. So far, project teams have started work in the Forest of Mercia (South Staffordshire), the Great North Forest (southern Tyne and Wear), Thames Chase (east of London) and Merseyside (especially at first around St Helens). Others are to come in Cleveland, Manchester, South Yorkshire, Nottingham, Bedford, Bristol, Swindon and South Hertfordshire. If there is one near you, find out about it. Start voluntary work in it if that is possible. Start birdwatching there and record the changes over the years as the forest grows (see Projects 48, 49 and 60). Write to the Countryside Commission for more information (for address, see page 125)

---

final say, and provides the money, so always let your Member of Parliament know of your conservation worries, or at a local level, tackle your local council. If enough of us lobby them, things do happen: derelict sites are brought back to life (as in St Helens, Lancashire, through the Groundwork Trust), and wild areas are managed as nature reserves within city boundaries.

We do not all have to do the same things. Some will tend a wildlife garden, others will write to their members of parliament; some will actively support a national pressure group, others will join a local natural history society; and some will simply support a 'green' stand at a county show, while others will volunteer their labour in a countryside management project.

Whatever we do, '...there is not the slightest justification for any smug, starry-eyed satisfaction that the world's wildlife is now safe in our enlightened hands'. So said Sir Frank Fraser Darling in the BBC's Reith lectures in 1969. How right he was! How right he is as you read this today! How right his word will still be in the days to come.

Opposite: a reserve of the Northumberland Naturalist's Trust on a stormy autumn afternoon, good for autumn migrants and winter wildfowl.
Above: *Unless we manage our land so that so-called weeds, such as teasels and dandelions, flourish we are in danger of losing a beautiful bird like the goldfinch.*

Making a Bird Garden

Conservation begins at home. Whether your garden is new or well established, it needs to be carefully planned and cared for if it is going to be attractive to birds.

Many a birdwatcher has been told by a friend, 'We don't get many birds in our garden!' The obvious reasons – noisy children, ill-trained dogs, cats – do deter birds, but a garden needs to be a suitable place for birds in the first place, and then it could record fifty or more species in a year.

In the wild, birds will naturally be sharing several major habitats. Of special interest to bird gardeners are the habitats of woodland edge, meadow and marshy pond. How much of any one of these three can be simulated in your garden depends on its size. Nevertheless, every effort should be made to create some woodland edge because it is true to say that garden birds are woodland birds. Some of the densest populations of birds are to be found in parks and built-up areas with their rich cover of shrubberies and broad-leaved trees. The greatest number of birds in natural woodland is to be found in broad-leaved or mixed woods, especially the typical English forest of oak, and its associated woodland edge shrubs and trees, such as hawthorn and holly.

Next, careful consideration should be given to the possibility of creating a pond with a shallow end so that birds can drink and bathe there (and so that insects may breed, including dragonflies). Also, a flowering meadow or flower border that is rich in

---

THE COMMONER WOODLAND BIRDS ARE THE MOST FAMILIAR GARDEN BIRDS

- Blue tit
- Great tit
- Chaffinch
- Wren
- Robin
- Blackbird
- Song thrush
- Dunnock
- Woodpigeon

The commoner woodland birds have adapted to our gardens. The one common woodland bird that has not made the transition is the willow warbler

---

blooms full of nectar for insects will in turn provide food for insectivorous birds (even throughout the year in the form of eggs and pupae). Finally, one should plan where to put a bird-table and bird-bath (*see* Project 19), where to have open ground to spread winter seed, where to put up nest boxes and where to plant evergreens for roosts.

SOME PLANTS YOU NEED IN A BIRD GARDEN

Many beautiful garden centre trees are sterile and are not suitable for a wildlife garden. Above is a list of plants that would serve your birds well.

GARDEN PLANTS FOR BIRDS

alder (if you have a damp corner, pond or stream)	S			
birch, silver	I	S		
blackberry	B	NS		
Cotoneaster (especially *horizontalis* or *wateri*)	B	I		
crab apple (not a yellow-fruiting form)	B			
dog rose	B	I		
elder	B	I		
gorse	I	NS		
hawthorn	B	I	NS	
holly	B	NS	R	
honeysuckle	B	NS	R	
ivy	B	I	NS	R
meadowsweet	I			
michaelmass daisies	I	S		
oak	I	NS	R	
pheasant bush	B			
rowan	B			
thistles	S			
'pussy' willow (i.e. the spring-flowering sallow)	N			
viburnam	R			
yew	B	NS	R	

Key (what the plants are good for) B=berries; I=insects; N=nectar; NS=nest site; R=roost; S=seeds.

The person who lives in a flat or is housebound may feel at a disadvantage when it comes to telling of the birds seen from the window. With probably no garden to call his own, and perhaps living several stories up, his chances of garden watching seem slim. However, it is amazing what can be trained to come to a window feeding station: a tit-feeder hung from a window frame and regular crumbs and seeds on a window-ledge can result in some fascinating watching. Tits will cross wide areas of open ground to come to a rich supply of food. I have seen them at a third story window about 100m (110 yds) from the nearest bush or tree. Many British towns now have collared doves and these will come to window-sills for seed, though they are not so tolerant of movement in the room as tits and chaffinches.

A development of the window-sill idea may be attempted by the erection of a birdwatcher's equivalent of a window-box, an approximately sized shallow tray screwed to the window-sill. The tray should be about 30–40cm (12–16in) wide, and have drainage holes in the base. Line the tray with sand and peat, either mixed or in an irregular mosaic pattern which looks attractive. This simulates soil and allows birds to dig in it. If starlings can be attracted to come, their digging can be watched and food-hunting success judged after a known quantity of mealworms or fat has been buried as bait. A blackbird may come and turn over specially laid leaves, as it would in the hedgerow, to find food beneath. If some twigs can be fixed for perches, these help because many species like to approach a table rather than land straight on it. A few plants can help create a miniature garden effect – you may be lucky and get a mallard nesting as has happened in the garden of one London flat!

Excellent, detailed help in creating a wildlife garden may be found in Gibbons (1988).

A garden needs to look, in some corners at least, as much like woodland edge as you can make it.

Major Habitat Conservation

A nature reserve is home to many birds. Your help is always needed to create or maintain private or official reserves in woodland, farms, churchyards, school grounds and wetlands.

In the ancient Bible story, God put man in charge of all creation. Nowadays, tales of soil erosion, of burning forests and recently extinct creatures abound. They are so dreadful that at last nations are worried about the survival of their own particular birds of the air and beasts of the field. Because of the immensity of the problem, no individual should say, 'But what can I do? I'm nobody special'. Each of us has some strength, time and talent, which could be devoted to helping make the world a better place. A splendidly detailed handbook for everyone keen to improve wildlife habitats is Baines and Smart's (1991) illustrated guide for wildlife gardeners, schools and local wildlife groups.

Over the years, lack of management and the gales of the late 1980s have left many woods in a sad state. Volunteers are often needed by County Naturalist Trusts, the Woodland Trust and the National Trust to help look after footpaths, clear brushwood, keep sunny rides and glades open, and do coppicing (for addresses *see* page 125). Each year, the National Trust and the Countryside Commission publish details of holiday camps for energetic volunteers who would be happy to tackle major projects.

Much has been written about the loss of habitat for birds on modern farmland. It has been argued more recently that the biggest change is not loss of hedges and copses, but farm management resulting in the disappearance of many mixed farms, that is farms that raise stock and grow crops. Song thrush, rook, skylark, lapwing, grey partridge and linnet have all suffered (but finches like rape fields, a recent

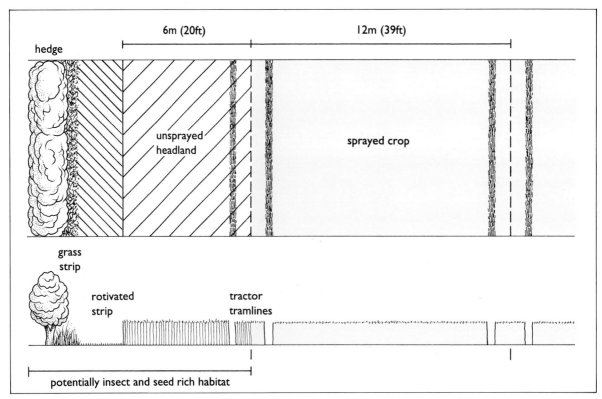

Recommendations for keeping unsprayed headlines around the edges of a field. This will encourage insect life and benefit grassland birds such as grey partridge.

PROJECT 59

A well-managed rather than a 'manicured' churchyard is a ready-made nature reserve. The mosaic of rough and mown grass, paths hedges, bushes and trees makes a haven for wildlife, whether the churchyard is in the middle of a busy town or in a more rural setting like this one on St Mary's in the Isles of Scilly, Cornwall.

phenomenon; study of that would make a good project). If you have the opportunity, discuss with a farmer the advantages of not spraying the edges (headlands) of fields, of creating a pond in a damp corner, and of allowing the junctions of hedgerows in particular to become wildlife havens by not harshly cutting them back.

If you do get to know a wood or farm well, contact the BTO to see if it would be helpful to do the Common Birds Census there (*see* Projects 48 and 49).

Many county birdwatching societies own reserves, or would like to. Manpower is always needed to trim hedges, clear ditches, plant trees, and raise money. Much good work is done by schools whose pupils help to maintain the grounds, paying special attention to encouraging feeding areas (such as teazles, thistles, fat hen and chickweed for finches) and maintaining nest sites (*see* Projects 5 and 6).

In villages, towns and cities throughout the land, thousands of chuchyards and cemeteries are (or potentially are) havens for wildlife because they are obvious refuges in an otherwise completely unsuitable environment. Most churchyards offer a mosaic of habitats: rough grassland, mown grass, paths, stonewalls, hedges, shrubs and trees. Carefully managed, with sympathy for wildlife, the churchyard can be full of flowers, insects and birds *and* a quiet, reflective place for congregation and visitors. All the grass need not be regularly mown like a lawn; all the flowers need not be in flower beds. Encouraged in this way, insects and seeds may flourish to attract spotted flycatchers and gold-

finch, blackcap and greenfinch. Maybe there are swifts, owls and bats in the tower which need special protection.

If you know a churchyard which would benefit from management for wildlife, get in touch with the vicar and the parochial church council (or the municipal council which looks after the cemetery). Discuss together the Living Churchyard project, which offers advice and grants in order that your aims may be realized. Full details may be obtained from the Church and Conservation Project of the National Agricultural Centre (for address *see* page 125), especially if you buy the DIY Information Pack.

Atlasing

An atlas of the birds of a given area takes many observers several years to produce, but results in a splendid tool for conservationists.

The spotted flycatcher is one of our more widespread breeding birds.

We have seen that there are now many special surveys which help to provide data for conservationists in their endeavours to protect habitats and particular species. But the activity above all which has been a feature of ornithology in the past twenty years is atlasing. Britain's detailed Ordnance Survey Maps have formed the basis of several marvelous publications. First there was *The Atlas of Breeding Birds in Britain and Ireland* (1976); then *The Atlas of Wintering Birds in Britain and Ireland* (1986); and, most recently, county maps for such widely spaced areas as Devon, Kent, Gwent and the Grampian Regions. A *New Atlas of Breeding Birds in Britain and Ireland* is in preparation, after several years' fieldwork.

The fieldwork is demanding

E	J	P	U	Z
D	I	N	T	Y
C	H	M	S	X
B	G	L	R	W
A	F	K	Q	V

THE BASIS OF ATLASING

A 10-km (6-mile) square is divided into a grid of 100 squares, each representing ground measuring 1 x 1km (0.6 x 0.6 miles). A square of 2 x 2km (1.2 x 1.2 miles; four small squares) is a tetrad. Each tetrad is coded with a letter for easy reference as above.

but it is very rewarding and fun, too. It satisfies our tick-hunting instincts, reveals surprises about 'common' species, and often delivers the 'prize' of discovering species hitherto unknown in the area. Instead of visiting only well-known haunts, the atlasing birdwatcher has to cover a given area methodically. In the original atlases, that given area was a 10-km (6-mile) square, which gave a rather coarse picture of distribution, especially at a local level. Only one breeding record per square was needed for each species. More recent atlases have been developed from even more demanding studies based on tetrads, which show the fine de-

SOME ATLASING STATISTICS

The Atlas of Breeding Birds in Britain and Ireland was published in 1976 after fieldwork:

- from 1968–1972 inclusive
- involving over 10,000 observers
- in all 3,682 10km squares in the UK were censused
- co-ordinated by about 200 organizers who collected 95,000 record cards
- which resulted in over 285,000 dots on the maps

The Tetrad Atlas of the Breeding Birds of Devon was published in 1988 after fieldwork:

- from 1977–1985
- involving over 300 observers
- in all of Devon's 1,834 tetrads
- giving 84,201 registrations (39,634 were of confirmed breeding) revealing one tetrad which had only a pair of rock pipits (and a lot of sea!) and another which had 85 species (65 proved to breed)
- showed 136 species bred of 147 seen
- all of which data was stored and made ready for printing thanks to a computer; the first time a county atlas had used such a machine.

tail of birds' distribution.

Generally, atlas helpers are asked to record 'Possible Breeding' (a bird seen in suitable nesting habitat), 'Probable Breeding' (a singing male, display or nest

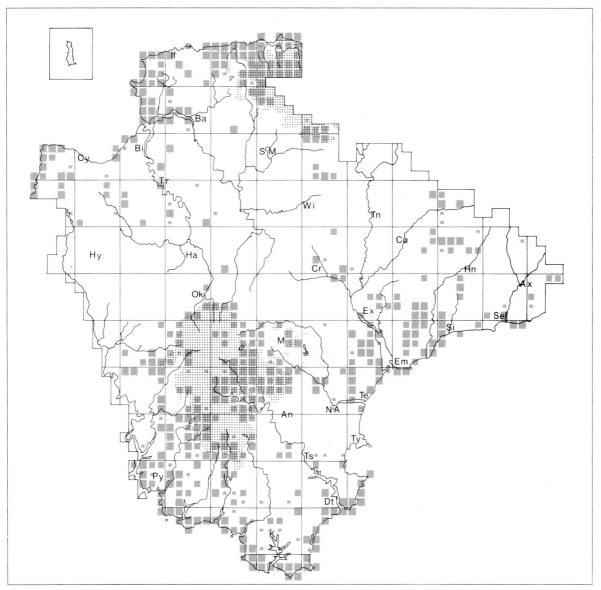

The stonechat map from The Tetrad Atlas of the Breeding Birds of Devon
shows clearly that it is a bird of Devon's heaths, moors and rough, coastal country.
Dartmoor is the shaded area in the bottom and Exmoor is at the top of the map.
The letters are abbreviations for the main towns (reproduced with permission).

building) or 'Confirmed Breeding' (nest with eggs or young, or adult feeding young). These observations are recorded on the map by small, medium or large dots respectively. Such a method shows only a bird's *distribution*, because a registration shows simply that a species bred at some time during the study period; it does not show how many pairs bred. At the time of writing, the BTO is compiling a new atlas using the tetrad technique which will show the relative abundance of species across Great Britain and Ireland. The Grampian atlas (Buckland *et al.*, 1990) shows both distribution and relative abundance and is Britain's first atlas based on all-year-round atlasing.

If you like the idea of searching all the nooks and crannies of your local patch, contact your local bird club to see what help they need.

Visiting Reserves

Holidays are the obvious times to visit nature reserves. We get a chance to go birdwatching in marshland, forest, moorland or on a sea-cliff which might be far from home.

Nature reserves provide ideal opportunities for seeing birds that are particularly associated with certain habitats. Many organizations are very conscious of the need to protect broad-leaved woods, chalk downs, reedbeds, moorland, marshes and seabird colonies. Such reserves are often wardened, provided with helpful literature, or have helpfully placed hides, and many have all three.

It behoves the visitor to find out in advance something about the reserve, besides what birds to see, so that no time is wasted.

Visiting is not the only activity a birdwatcher can do at a reserve. The RSPB needs voluntary wardens every year. Contact them if you think you can help. County Naturalists Trusts, the National Trust, the Woodland Trust and local ornithological societies welcome helpers, too, as guides, regular observers or labourers with muscle to work on the site.

Information about reserves and nature trails can be obtained from the *Where to Watch Birds ...* series published by Christopher Helm, the British Tourist Board, and the societies named above.

POINTS TO CONSIDER WHEN VISITING A RESERVE

- How do I get there?
- Is there a car park?
- Can I leave my bike somewhere safe?
- Do I have to pay on entry or obtain a permit in advance?
- Does the best watching depend on tides?
- Are there any guided walks to take advantage of?
- Is there a daily log book in which to write my observations?
- Who is the county bird recorder? (see Project 64.)

Your paying for a visit, or working there in some way, will each help to keep the reserve going.

The Bird of Prey Viewpoint on Haldon Hill, Devon, is a joint venture between the RSPB, Forestry Commission and the Devon Birdwatching and Preservation Society. Up to seven species of raptors have been seen from here on one day.

Special Species Surveys

For many a birdwatcher, the more he knows, the more he realizes what there is still to be discovered.

Many birdwatchers come to admit they have a favourite bird, or at least a couple from very different families. With some, the interest develops into a passion and results in many hours a year, and many years, being spent studying the life of that species. That personal interest and satisfying of curiosity is shared sometimes with a friend or at a society lecture (*see* Project 65). With others the interest develops so strongly and is pursued so scientifically that the results become a whole book of general interest to most birdwatchers. The first monograph really to stir others to the same task was David Lack's *The Life of the Robin*, which first ap-

peared in 1943 and ran to four editions over the course of the next twenty years or so. No one has bettered that, although many have tried (*see* Project 54).

Studies of individual species are organized by bird clubs and societies. In this way the birdwatcher's interest is immediately channelled into activity which probably has an immediate conservation slant. Enquiries into the status of the woodlark, cirl bunting, barn owl, Dartford warbler and wood warbler have all been of national importance in recent years.

If you are keen to provide information to be used to further protective measures for a species,

contact your local ornithological club or the BTO to find out what is being surveyed.

Status of the grey heron in Great Britain from the Heronries Census.

THE HERONRIES CENSUS

- This was started by the BTO in 1928.
- It is the BTO's longest-running population monitoring scheme.
- Annual counts from a sample of heronries are available from 1928 and produce an annual population index.
- These simple counts have been augmented by complete counts in 1928, 1954, 1964 and 1965.
- All these counts provide the longest continuous series of population figures for any European breeding bird.

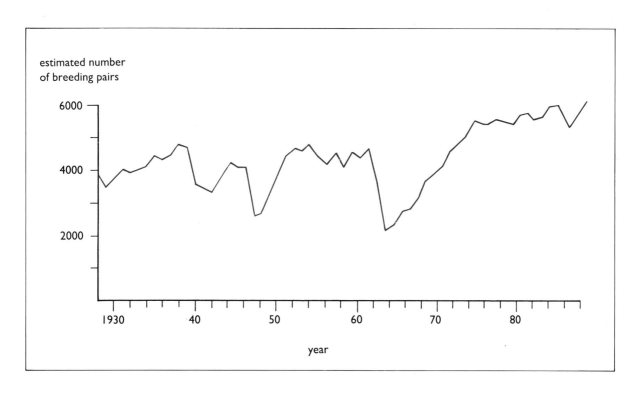

Birds of Waterways

There is much concern for the continued existence of watery habitats throughout the world. Conservation of our rivers must be a vital part of our birdwatching.

One of the glories of our countryside is the river: tumbling hill stream, haunt of grey wagtails and dippers; slow, lowland river with its chirping reed buntings and watchful kingfishers; broad estuary alive with gulls and shorebirds. All are threatened: dippers are known to be declining in Wales where streams are so acidic now that there is not enough invertebrate food; the 'management' of our lowland streams by straightening channels and clearing vegetation affects several species including the kingfisher; and plans for marinas, barrages and industries on estuaries are of grave concern to those who fear for our nationally and internationally important wintering flocks of waders and wildfowl.

Two important BTO surveys have great potential as tools for conservation of our waterways:

the Waterways Survey and Birds of the Estuaries Enquiry (BoEE).

The Waterways Survey began in 1974. It aims to provide an annual index of the population levels of nineteen species not already covered by the Common Birds Census; and data on habitat requirements and regional distribution is needed to assess the effect of waterways management and pollution on riparian (i.e. riverside) birds.

A suitable waterway to survey would be a section of a canal or river (not a tidal or partly tidal stretch) at least 3km (2 miles) long. The observer promises to visit the river nine or ten times during the breeding season between mid-March and mid-July. Your river may include only a few of these species, but regular watching will surely reveal many other birds of interest to you and your local bird recorder: goos-

anders, sand martins and reed warblers, perhaps.

On each visit the birds seen are plotted on a 6in : 1 mile (1 : 10,560 or 1 : 10,000) scale map. At the end of the season, all the maps are transferred to 'species maps' and are sent to the BTO for analysis.

Only a little over a hundred observers take part each year. Some regions of the country are poorly served. Birdwatchers are particularly urged to start a WBS on an upland river at risk from acidification. With improved observer coverage and habitat-recording techniques, the survey should become an even more valuable aid to conservation.

THE WATERWAYS BIRD SURVEY (WBS) BIRDS

Little grebe	Mute swan
Mallard	Tufted duck
Moorhen	Coot
Oystercatcher	Lapwing
Curlew	Redshank
Common	Kingfisher
sandpiper	Yellow wagtail
Grey wagtail	Dipper
Sedge warbler	Whitethroat
Reed bunting	

Story of a reed bunting registration. (1) A reed bunting is seen singing near a bridge on visit B, the scene of a fight between two moorhens. The bird flies across the river and resumes singing. A second male is then heard singing against the first. (2) All this information is entered on the visit map, using symbols and codes. (3) At the end of the season, reed bunting registrations from all visits are transferred to a reed bunting species map. Song registrations from visit B now appear as 'B' on the species map. The map is analysed by the BTO where the registrations near the bridge are awarded one territory.

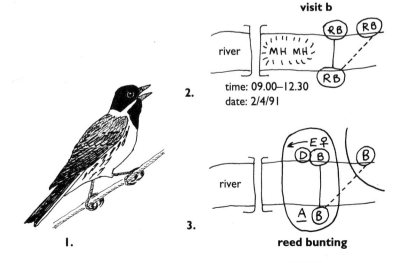

reed bunting

1.

Birds of Estuaries

The thousands of miles of coastline and the many estuaries of the British Isles are vital to the survival of hundreds of thousands of Europe's waders and wildfowl.

The BoEE is supported by over a thousand observers, controlled by local organizers. Counts are made once a month and have been made throughout the land since 1969. The British and Irish coastline is of international importance as a habitat for wintering waders and wildfowl (*see* Project 47). About half of all the waders that winter in Europe in the intertidal zone are found on our shores and in our estuaries. Therefore the BTO and all its helpers (together with co-sponsors, the RSPB, DoENI and the JNCC) have a great incentive to know more about the environ-

ment in order to conserve it. Already, many sites owe their protection directly to the efforts of BoEE counters.

The counts are carried out simultaneously on all British estuaries and many coastal sites on pre-selected dates which have been chosen to coincide with spring tides. On small estuaries, counting is not too much of a problem, but on larger estuaries observers need to count the waders when they are going to roost, whilst at the roost, or as they leave. If you are not used to counting large numbers of birds, you should go out with an

SOME BoEE FACTS

- During the period of the enquiry, grey plover numbers have more than doubled (to over 37,000).

- Dunlin have declined by about a third (to around 450,000).

- An increasing number of requests is received each year for information to work out the implications of coastal developments. This clearly shows the enquiry's worth. The biggest task at present is to try to assess what a barrage (a dam to produce electricity) across the River Severn would do to its 50,000 wintering waders which includes Britain's second largest population of Dunlin.

- Over a million and a half waders of over thirty species are recorded each year by the BoEE.

experienced birdwatcher several times before you take on an estuary to survey yourself.

Participants in the enquiry receive free the annual report publishing the season's results and regular newsletters.

Both of these BTO enquiries deserve good support. They add purpose and interest to a day's birdwatching. If you believe you can help, write to the BTO (for address *see* page 125) well before the season starts; new counters are always welcome and their contributions much appreciated.

Ynys-hir and the Dovey Estuary, mid-Wales, an RSPB reserve and haunt of many waders and wildfowl.

Writing a Note or Paper

All those observations stored in notebook, sketchbook and computer need a wider audience. The more you watch, the more you are likely to know something that is worth publishing

Perhaps the most important piece of writing a birdwatcher should do is his records which he should send in every year to the recorders of the county or regional birdwatching societies. These societies report on the areas for which he has observations. These records are welcomed from members and non-members alike. County recorders are volunteers who compile annual reports in their spare time. Your records should therefore be typed, word-processed or neatly written on one side of the paper only so that the recorder does not have to waste any time reading your submission. Send in your records in an orderly, methodical way. Firstly, copy out in rough from your notes all the records you wish to pass on. Then write them out properly, in systematic order, using a previous annual report or a field guide to get the species in order. Many records will need just species name, locality, date and number of birds. Other records will need to have added behavioural details, or plumage description for uncommon or rare birds (your local society will probably have its own list with which you should become familiar). (*See* also page 124 for national rarities all of which will be checked and accepted by experts before publication is made.)

Later, when you feel confident you have some original observations or research which you think deserves publishing, you should look at previous issues of magazines to see the way other authors have presented their work. Major publications such as *British Birds* and *Bird Study* print guide-lines for authors on the inside cover of each issue.

SOME SAMPLE RECORDS READY TO SEND AWAY

Blackbird   Gore's copse 7.04
    one complete albino, save for dark eye and normal bright yellow bill, legs flesh coloured.

Fieldfare Liddington Hill   30.04
    last of the season.
        Fox Hill   18.10
    nine on hawthorn; first for the winter.

Song thrush Yealmpton 20.05
    singing between 22.00 and 23.00 by the light of a street lamp. Also 01, 07 and 10.06

Cetti's warbler Rumleigh
        04.04   one singing
        05.05   two singing
        16.05   two singing
        10.06   one with food
        08.10   one singing
        24.12   one singing

HINTS ON WRITING A PAPER

Plan the paper with an introduction, sections on previous work (do your homework! Do not waste the editor's time by printing something as new, which repeats information that is known already), your methods of study, results, discussion, acknowledgements, bibliography and summary.

Compose the paper carefully, with at least one if not two drafts. Ask another birdwatcher to read it, criticise it and be honest!

Take care with scientific names, text figures, maps, tables, photographs and references. Every magazine has its own conventional style: check it before you send off your manuscript.

Be prepared for more criticism, rejection, re-writing, and proof-reading if you are lucky and it does go to print!

If you had watched this serin in Britain you would need to write a detailed description of it as a rare bird for your local bird report, and a detailed account of its bathing and preening.

PROJECT 66

Join a Society

Finally, a good birdwatcher shares his or her experiences with friends. A good hobby costs something, and some of that cost should go on a subscription to a bird club.

So we have come full circle, back to the notebook. In theory it is now full of facts of ornithological interest, and may well contain so much that a new one or a refill will have to be used next year. What is to happen to these notes?

Some birdwatchers, even eminent professionals, have stated publically that their birdwatching is fun for them and is nobody else's business. Although the hobby is not technically a team game I do feel that this point of view is not a good one, because far more fun and satisfaction can be forthcoming if knowledge and experiences are shared. If a bird-watcher sends his records to his local birdwatching society, knowledge of the avifauna of the area covered by its report may be as complete as possible; he may in turn gain further knowledge from its contents. Most local birdwatching societies have regular indoor and field meetings, which provide valuable opportunities for contacting folk of like mind, all keen to increase their knowledge of a fascinating hobby. The books by Bob Scott (1987) and John Gooders (1988) describe hundreds of places where birdwatching is good; the series of county birdwatching guides published by Christopher Helm give even more detail. If you wish to contact local bird society secretaries named there or in other books, check at the public library, where there should be copies of the local society's latest reports, containing a list of present officers.

National organizations whose sphere of influence and work would benefit from more active support, and who have all helped in the writing of this book, are the British Trust for Ornithology (BTO);

British Trust for Ornithology

the International Council for Bird Preservation (ICBP);

the Royal Society for the Protection of Birds (RSPB);

and the Wildfowl and Wetlands Trust (WWT).

THE WILDFOWL & WETLANDS TRUST

Addresses for all these organizations are given on page 125. To belong to more than one organization may be expensive. Start with a local subscription. Later, a working birdwatcher should not begrudge at least a subscription each to a local and a national body.

And the point of it all? Perhaps no more than has been so finely put by Michael Hamburger in this extract from his poem *Birdwatcher*:

Challenged he'd say it was a
    mode of knowing ...
Darkly aware that like his
    opposite
Who no less deep in woods,
    as far out on moors
Makes do with food or
    trophies, hunts for easy
    favours,
He trysts defeat by what he
    cannot know.

Even when someone knows all the answers to all the questions in this book, the answers will have made him ask more questions – the challenge to know more will remain.

List of Species Considered by the *British Birds* Rarities Committee (BBRC)

The following species, and also any that would be new to Category A of the British and Irish list, are considered by the BBRC. Details of some well-marked subspecies (for example teal of the North American race *Anas crecca carolinensis*, yellow wagtail of the black-headed race *Motacilla flava feldegg*) are also required.

White-bellied diver
Pied-billed grebe
Black-browed albatross
Capped petrel
Bulwer's petrel
Little shearwater
Wilson's petrel
White-faced petrel
Madeiran petrel
Magnificent frigatebird
American bittern
Little bittern
Night heron
Green heron
Squacco heron
Cattle egret
Great white egret
Black stork
Glossy ibis
Lesser white-fronted goose
Red-breasted goose
American wigeon
Baikal teal
Black duck
Blue-winged teal
Red-necked duck
King eider
Steller's eider
Harlequin duck
Bufflehead
Hooded merganser
Black kite
White-tailed eagle
Egyptian vulture
Griffon vulture
Pallid harrier
Spotted eagle
Lesser kestrel
American kestrel
Red-footed falcon
Eleonora's falcon
Gyr falcon
Sora rail
Little crake
Baillon's crake
Allen's gallinule

American purple gallinule
American coot
Sandhill crane
Little bustard
Houbara bustard
Great bustard
Black-winged stilt
Cream-coloured courser
Collared pratincole
Semipalmated plover
Killdeer
Greater sand plover
Caspian plover
American golden plover
Pacific golden plover
Sociable plover
White-tailed plover
Semipalmated sandpiper
Western sandpiper
Red-necked stint
Long-toed stint
Lesser sandpiper
White-rumped sandpiper
Baird's sandpiper
Sharp-tailed sandpiper
Broad-billed sandpiper
Stilt sandpiper
Great snipe
Short-billed dowitcher
Long-billed dowitcher
Hudsonian godwit
Little whimbrel
Eskimo curlew
Upland sandpiper
Marsh sandpiper
Greater yellowlegs
Lesser yellowlegs
Solitary sandpiper
Terek sandpiper
Spotted sandpiper
Grey-tailed tattler
Wilson's phalarope
Great black-headed gull

Laughing gull
Franklin's gull
Bonaparte's gull
Slender-billed gull
Ross's gull
Gull-billed tern
Caspian tern
Royal tern
Lesser crested tern
Aleutian tern
Forster's tern
Bridled tern
Sooty tern
Whiskered tern
White-winged black tern
Brünnich's guillemot
Pallas's sandgrouse
Rufous turtle dove
Great spotted cuckoo
Black-billed cuckoo
Scops owl
Eagle owl
Snowy owl
Hawk owl
Tengmalm's owl
Red-necked nightjar
Egyptian nightjar
Common nighthawk
Needle-tailed swift
Chimney swift
Pallid swift
Pacific swift
Alpine swift
Little swift
Belted kingfisher
Blue-cheeked bee-eater
Roller
Yellow-bellied sapsucker
Calandra lark
Bimaculated lark
White-winged lark
Short-toed lark
Lesser short-toed lark
Crested lark
Red-rumped swallow
Cliff swallow
Blyth's pipit
Olive-backed pipit
Pechora pipit
Red-throated pipit
American pipit
Citrine wagtail
Alpine accentor
Rufous bush robin
Thrush nightingale
Siberian rubythroat

Red-flanked bluetail
White-throated robin
Isabelline wheatear
Pied wheatear
Black-eared wheatear
Desert wheatear
White-crowned black wheatear
Black wheatear
Rock thrush
White's thrush
Siberian thrush
Hermit thrush
Swainson's thrush
Grey-cheeked thrush
Veery
Eye-browed thrush
Dusky thrush
Black-throated thrush
American robin
Fan-tailed warbler
Pallas's grasshopper warbler
Lanceolated warbler
River warbler
Moustached warbler
Paddyfield warbler
Blyth's reed warbler
Great reed warbler
Thick-billed warbler
Olivaceous warbler
Booted warbler
Marmora's warbler
Spectacled warbler
Subalpine warbler
Sardinian warbler
Rüppell's warbler
Desert warbler
Orphean warbler
Green warbler
Greenish warbler
Arctic warbler
Radde's warbler
Dusky warbler
Bonelli's warbler
Collared flycatcher
Wallcreeper
Short-toed treecreeper
Penduline tit
Brown shrike
Isabelline shrike
Lesser grey shrike
Nutcracker
Daurian starling
Rose-coloured starling
Spanish sparrow
Rock sparrow
Philadelphia vireo

Red-eyed vireo
Citril finch
Arctic redpoll
Two-barred crossbill
Parrot crossbill
Trumpeter finch
Pine grosbeak
Evening grosbeak
Black-and-white warbler
Tennesee warbler
Parula warbler
Yellow warbler
Chestnut-sided warbler
Cape may warbler
Magnolia warbler
Yellow-rumped warbler
Blackpoll warbler
American redstart
Ovenbird
Northern waterthrush
Yellowthroat
Hooded warbler
Wilson's warbler
Summer tanager
Scarlet tanager
Rufous-sided towhee
Savannah sparrow
Fox sparrow
Song sparrow
White-crowned sparrow
White-throated sparrow
Dark-eyed junco
Pine bunting
Rock bunting
Cretzschmer's bunting
Yellow-browed bunting
Rustic bunting
Little bunting
Yellow-breasted bunting
Pallas's reed bunting
Black-headed bunting
Rose-breasted grosbeak
Indigo bunting
Bobolink
Northern oriole

Addresses for Birdwatchers

The Barn Owl Trust, Waterleat, Ashburton, Devon TQ13 7HU

Birdline, 24-hour telephone service 0898 700241

British Birds, Fountains, Park Lane, Blunham, Bedford MK44 3NJ

The British Trust for Ornithology (BTO), The Nunnery, Nunnery Place, Thetford, Norfolk IP24 2PU

The Countryside Commission, John Dower House, Crescent Place, Cheltenham, Gloustershire GL50 3RA.

Foreign Birdwatching Reports and Information Service (FBRIS), 5 Stanway Close, Blackpole, Worcester WR4 9XL

Gauntlett, S.J.M, 'Tickers', High Street, Cley-next-the-Sea, Holt, Norfolk NR25 7RR for lists for Kenya, southern Africa, Majorca, Israel and Greece

The Hawk and Owl Trust, c/o Zoological Society of London, Regent's Park, London NW1 4RY

International Council for Bird Preservation (ICBP), 32 Cambridge Road, Girton, Cambridge CB3 0PJ

Living Churchyard Project, c/o National Agricultural Centre, Stoneleigh, Warwickshire CV8 2LZ

National Bird News, 24-hour telephone service 0898 884500

The National Trust, 36 Queen Anne's Gate, London SW1H 9AS

Natural Environment Research Council (NERC), Polaris House, North Star Avenue, Swindon, Wiltshire

NatureBASE, Holbrook House, 105 Rose Hill, Oxford OX4 4HT

OBSERVATORIES

Bardsey Island, c/o Mrs H. Bond, 21a Gestridge Road, Kingsteignton, Devon

Calf of Man, c/o Mrs M. Kennaugh, Manx Museum, Douglas, Isle of Man

Cape Clear, c/o Mr O. O'Sullivan, 46 The Glen, Boden Park, Dublin 14, Eire

Copeland, c/o Mr N.D. Mckee, 67 Temple Rise, Templepatrick, County Antrim BT39 0AG

The Warden, Dungeness Bird Observatory, Romney Marsh, Lydd, Kent

The Warden, Gibraltar Point Field Centre, Skegness, Lincolnshire

The Warden, Fair Isle Bird Observatory, Fair Isle, Shetland ZE2 9JU

Isle of May, c/o Mrs. R. Cowper, 9 Oxgangs Road, Edinburgh EH10 7BG

North Ronaldsay, c/o Dr K. Woodbridge, Twinsness, North Ronaldsay, Orkney KW7 2BE

Mr M. Rogers, Portland Bird Observatory, Old Lower Light, Portland, Dorset

The Warden, Sandwich Bay Bird Observatory, Old Downs Farm, Guildford Road, Sandwich Bay, Sandwich, Kent CT13 9PF

The Warden, Spurn Bird Observatory, Kilnsea via Patrington, Hull HU12 0UG

The Warden, Walney Bird Observatory, Coastguard Cottages, South Walney, Barrow-in-Furness, Cumbria LA14 3YQ

Operation Swift, c/o S. Keightley, PO Box 29, Boston, Lincolnshire PE21 0NL

Ornitholidays, 1–3 Victoria Drive, Bognor Regis, West Sussex PO21 2PW

Rarities Committee, c/o *British Birds*, Fountains, Park Lane, Blunham, Bedford MK44 3NJ.

Royal Society for Nature Conservation (RSNC) (The Wildlife Trusts Partnership), The Green, Witham Park, Waterside South, Lincoln LN2 7JR

Royal Society for the Prevention of Cruelty to Animals (RSPCA), phone one of their Oiled Seabird Units at once:
  (a) National Wildlife Unit, West Hatch, near Taunton, Somerset (0823 480156)
  (b) Animal Welfare Centre, Perranporth, Cornwall (0872 573856)
  (c) Oiled Seabird Unit, Plymouth, Devon (0752 405475)
  (d) Oiled Seabird Unit, Torquay, Devon (0803 294253)

Royal Society for the Protection of Birds (RSPB), The Lodge, Sandy, Bedfordshire SG19 2DL

Seabirds Team, Joint Nature Conservation Committee, Wynne-Edwards House, 16–17 Rubislaw Terrace, Aberdeen AB1 1XE

Wildfowl and Wetlands Trust, Slimbridge, Gloucester GL2 7BT

Bibliography

Armstrong, E.A. (1947) *Bird Display and Behaviour.*

Armstrong, E.A. (1955) *The Wren.*

Atkinson-Willes, G. (1964) *Count.* In Thomson, A.L. (ed) *A New Dictionary of Birds.*

Austin, O. (1961) *Birds of the World.*

Baines, C. & Smart, J. (1991) *Guide to Habitat Creation.*

Bannerman, D. (1953) *The Birds of the British Isles,* **2**.

Barnard, C. & Thompson, D. (1985) *Gulls and Plovers.*

Barrett, J. & Yonge, C.M. (1958) *Pocket Guide to the Sea Shore.*

Betts, M.M. (1955) The behaviour of a pair of great tits. *British Birds,* **48**, 77–82.

Brooks-King, M. & Hurrell, H.G. (1958) Intelligence Tests with Tits. *British Birds,* **51**, 514–24.

Brooks-King, M. (1955) What song is that? *Devon Birds,* **24**, 3–4.

Brown, P.E. & Wolfendale, R. (1948) An exercise in the recording of bird song. *Bird Notes,* **23**, 133–6.

Brown, L. (1955) *Eagles.*

Burton, R. (1985) *Bird Behaviour.*

Buxton, J. (1950) *The Redstart.*

Campbell, B. & Lack, E. (eds) (1984) *A Dictionary of Birds.*

Catchpole, C. (1981) Why do birds sing? *New Scientist,* **2**, 29–31.

Coward, T.A. (1950) *The Birds of the British Isles and their Eggs* (First Series*).*

Cowie, R. & Hinsley, S. (1988) The Provision of food and the use of bird feeders in suburban gardens. *Bird Study,* **35**, 163–8.

Cramp, S. (ed) (1988) *The Birds of the Western Palaearctic,* Volume V.

Cramp, S. *et al.* (1974) *The Seabirds of Britain and Ireland.*

Darwin, C. (1901) *A Naturalist's Voyage Round The World* (Second Edition).

Davidson, N.C. *et al.* (1986) Why do Curlews *Numerius* have decurved bills? *Bird Study,* **33**, 61–9.

Diamond, A.W. (1987) *Save The Birds.*

Fisher, J. (1952) *The Fulmar.*

Fisher, J. (1954) *A History of Birds.*

Gibb, J. & Hartley, P.H.T. (1957) Bird Foods and Feeding Habits as Subjects for amateur research. *British Birds,* **50**, 278–91.

Gibbons, B. & L. (1988) *Creating a Wildlife Garden.*

Gooders, J. (1988) *Where to Watch Birds in Britain and Europe.*

Goodfellow, P. (1971) *The Birds of Saltram – Past and Present.*

Goodfellow, P. (1977) *Birds as Builders.*

Grant, P.J. (1986) *Gulls: A Guide To Identification* (second edition).

Harrison, P. (1983) *Seabirds: An Identification Guide.*

Hartley, P.H.T. (1954) Wild fruits in the diet of British thrushes. *British Birds,* **47**, 97–107.

Hendriksuna, J.T. (1964) Protecting ground nests from cattle. *British Birds,* **57**, 189–90.

Hill, M. & Langsbury, G. (1988) *A Field Guide to Photographing Birds in Britain and Western Europe.*

Hollom, P.A.D. (1952) *The Popular Handbook of British Birds.*

Kay, Q.O.N. (1985) Nectar from willow catkins as a food source for Blue Tits. *Bird Study,* **32**, 40–44.

Kirby, J.S. *et al* (1990) *Wildfowl and Wader Counts 1989-1990.*

Lack, D. (1965) *The Life of the Robin* (fourth edition).

Lemaire, F. (1979) Mimicry in the song of the Marsh Warbler. *Ibis,* **121**, 453–68.

Lloyd, C.S. *et al.* (1991) *The Status of Seabirds in Britain and Ireland.*

Löfgren, L. (1984) *Ocean Birds: Their Breeding, Biology and Behaviour.*

Lorenz, K.Z. (1952) *King Solomon's Ring.*

Mayer-Gross, H. (1964) Late nesting in Britain in 1960. *British Birds,* **57**, 102–118.

Mead, C.J. & Clark, J.A. (1990) Report on Bird Ringing for Britain and Ireland for 1989. *Ringing & Migration,* **11**, 137–176.

Mountfort, G. (1957) *The Hawfinch.*

Nelson, B. (1968) *Galapagos Island of Birds.*

Nelson, B. (1978) *The Gannet.*

Nicholson, E.M. (1959) Special Review: Bird numbers in Finland. *British Birds,* **52**, 22–30.

O'Connor, R. & Shrubb, M. (1986) *Farming and Birds.*

Ormerod, S.J. & Tyler, S.J. (1988) The diet of Green Sandpipers in contrasting areas of their winter range. *Bird Study,* **35**, 25–30.

Penwarden, Mr & Mrs C.B. (1969) The Bird Table Census. *Devon Birds,* **22**, no. 4.

Percy, Lord William (1951) *Three Studies in Bird Character.*

Perrins, C. (1979) *British Tits.*

Scott, B. (1987) *The Atlas of British Birdlife.*

Sharpe, R.B. (1896) *Wonders of the Bird World.*

Simmons, K.E.L. (1955) Studies on Great Crested Grebes. *The Agricultural Magazine,* **61**.

Simms, E. (1971) *Woodland Birds.*

Smith, S. & Hosking, E. (1955) *Birds Fighting.*

Soper, T. (1986) *The Bird Table Book.*

Snow, D.W. (1958) *A Study of Blackbirds.*

Snow, D. & B. (1988) *Birds and Berries.*

Sparks, J. & Soper, T. (1970) *Owls, Their Natural and Unnatural History.*

Summers-Smith, D. (1963) *The House Sparrow.*

Tinbergen, N. & Falkus, H. (1970) *Signals for Survival.*

Waite, R.K. (1985) Food catching and recovery by farmland corvids. *Bird Study,* **32**, 45–49.

Walsh, P.M. *et al.* (1991) Seabird Numbers and Breeding Success in 1990. *Nature Conservancy Council CSD Report* no. 1235.

White, Rev G. (1789) *The Natural History of Selbourne.*

Willughby, F. & Ray, J. (1978) *Ornithology* (in the Paul Muriet Fascimile Edition, 1972).

Yapp, W.B. (1962) *Birds and Woods.*

Index

Page numbers in *italic* refer to illustrations.

Photographic Acknowledgements

Photographs by the author except for those on the pages indicated below.
Roger Aldersley 108; David Goodfellow 35, 85, 94, 109 (bottom left); Robin Khan 118; Muzz Murray (Barn Owl Trust) 57; **Nature Photographers Ltd** 79 (Frank Blackburn), 122 (Mark Bolton), 63 (Kevin Carlson), 29 (Colin Carver), 36 (Hugh Clark), 9 (Andrew Cleave), 30 (Geoff du Feu), 71, 88 (M.R. Hill), 19, 52, 101 (E.A. Janes), 15, 31, 111 (Paul Sterry), 11, 64, 69, 78, 93 (Roger Tidman), 50 (Maurice Walker); **Natural Image** 41, 121 (Bob Gibbons), 36, 40, 69 (Mike Lang), 60 (J. Poole), 36, 43, 47, 116 (Peter Wilson); Ken Partridge 102; Peter Rock 97; M. Turpitt 109 (top right); Steve Whitehouse 109 (top left).